Thomas Dellenbusch

Hidden in Her Heart
A Novella

Thomas Dellenbusch
"HIDDEN IN HER HEART"

Already published:

Thomas Dellenbusch
"CHASE: The Hunt for the Mute Poetess"
ISBN 978-3-9817967-4-2
"CHASE: The Hunt for a King"
ISBN 978-3-9817967-9-7

First Publication in German 2014
First Publication in English 2017
All Rights Reserved
2014 Thomas Dellenbusch

Proofreading and typesetting: Kopfkino Publishing
Cover Design: coverandbooks / Rica Aitzetmüller
Cover Theme: © Masson / Shutterstock
Translated by Richard Urmston, Impressum Translators
Printed by: Createspace.com

Kopfkino-Verlag
Thomas Dellenbusch
Gluckstrasse 10
40724 Hilden
GERMANY

ISBN 978-3-9818651-2-7

www.Movie-Length-Stories.com

Thomas Dellenbusch

HIDDEN IN HER HEART

A NOVELLA

About KopfKino:

Kopfkino ("Theatre of the Mind") offers touching, thought-provoking and enthralling **movie-length-stories** with an approximate reading-time of between 60 and 180 minutes.

They're perfect for all of those daily interludes: a trip on the train, bus, car or plane, the hours spent in waiting-rooms or at the hairdresser's, on your coffee-break, during an afternoon at the beach, before turning out the lights at bedtime, or simply "in-between." Everything you need to fill 1, 2 or 3 hours in a most entertaining way.

Because the reading-times are virtually the same as the length of the average movie, they're great for couples or groups to read aloud to each other—and to switch off the TV for a change. Don't let the tube and the big screen monopolize your leisure time.

Create pictures, from the sentimental to the thrilling, on the world's greatest silver screen of all: your fantasy!

Every story is available in both Kindle eBook and audiobook format; many can also be purchased as paperbacks.

Keep yourself up-to-date with:
Movie-Length-Stories.com
for new releases, author bios, live-reading dates,
general information, or to download individual
stories in eBook or audiobook format.

1

There was no hairdresser in Seilersfeld. The sleepy little village, located between Landshut and Passau in Lower Bavaria, with only eight hundred inhabitants, had only a bakery, a tavern cum inn and a small grocery store, which offered a modest range of drugstore and household items as well as stationery. Public facilities were almost non-existent, apart from the parish church, located in a community hall, a grammar school with an adjoining kindergarten, and a small-town hall—on the ground floor of which was the office of Hubert Förster, Seilersfeld's district commissioner of the police department.

For everything else, such as a hair salon for example, Seilersfeld was simply too small. The women of the village had to drive to the county seat to have their hair done up in an elaborate coiffure for those special occasions like weddings, baptisms or funerals where it was necessary. When it came to everyday hair-care, however, most of them called on Birgit Förster, the wife of the village sheriff, as her husband was affectionately called by the villagers.

Birgit Förster had been a trained hairdresser. She'd given up her job in a salon at the county seat when she got pregnant for the first time and her husband took up his post as police commissioner at Seilersfeld's town hall. Now she offered her skills to the local women in her own kitchen and in so doing was able to augment the household income.

There was another, very practical reason why hairdresser appointments in the city were rare. In the early sixties, very few women in Germany had a driver license. In Seilersfeld, there was not a single one. In addition, not many of the villagers owned a vehicle. The Berggruber Bakery had a small van, used for the business. The Kranz family, the owners of the grocery store, and the Heuslingers who operated the tavern/inn, each had a car, but the number of private cars in Seilersfeld at that time was still very small.

This afternoon, Hilde Kranz, her son Bernd and the bakery's Ruth Berggruber, were sitting in the small kitchen of the policeman's wife/hairdresser. For the sixteen-year-old high school student, these gatherings at Frau Förster's were not just dead boring, but also exasperating: for months now he had been wishing he could get a moptop haircut just like the famed Beatles from England. And although he once had wheedled a half-hearted "It's all right with me" out of his father, his mother still vehemently vetoed this literally hair-raising idea.

As a result, the young man had to deal with his frustration when Frau Förster cut his hair to the length that jutted out over the short teeth of her comb. So, after a hopeful and anticipatory period of growth, once again he ended up with neatly-exposed ears and an accurately drawn side-part. So, Michl Holzgärtner would remain the only boy in the village who was allowed to wear a Beatles haircut. After all, he was a farmer, or rather, he was the sixteen-year-old offspring of the farmer Gustl Holzgärtner. And a farm boy's appearance was not something that had to pass middle-class muster. In addition, his moptop hairstyle looked that way simply because he only occasionally got a haircut; thus, his head looked rather like an actual mop. Therefore, he was not viewed by the parents of his peers as a pioneer of a new and—for that reason alone —repulsive fashion, but simply as what he was. A farmer.

This afternoon, though, Bernd "Berni" Kranz for once didn't fight his boredom and frustration. On the contrary. He feared that his heightened interest in the conversation of the three women might be revealed unintentionally by the sudden and intense reddening of his earlobes. He strove, therefore, to put on the same bored expression he usually presented in Frau Forster's kitchen. They were talking about the new arrival in the village.

Three weeks ago, she'd moved into the extension that Gustl Holzgärtner had built onto his own house many years ago for his aging parents. After his widowed mother died, the building, which had a separate entrance, had remained uninhabited. Now someone was living there again.

Since the end of May.

The new woman in the village.

Yvonne Schmidt.

And this Yvonne Schmidt quickly became the topic of intensive conversations around the village among adults—and at the same time of late-night fantasies of adolescent boys such as Berni Kranz.

On her first day in Seilersfeld she strutted through the town in high heel shoes, which made her long, slender legs appear even more elongated. Those legs were covered only minimally by a blue-and-white mottled dress whose hem barely reached her knees and, being extremely tight, emphasized her swinging hips and the apple-like roundness of her buttocks. The worst (or most exciting, depending on one's point of view) was what presented itself above the waistline.

A willowy waist widened to a significant, solid and prominent bust, whose ability to draw attention was surpassed only by the youthful beauty of a face such as the young in Seilersfeld had never seen—and the old had only ever seen in the movies.

Large, dark-brown eyes, together with a delicate nose, clear and slightly tanned skin, high cheekbones and full red lips, made for an angelic face, which was complemented by an open mane full of black hair, which spilled over her shoulders and back in natural waves.

The first impression on that first day many of the villagers in Seilersfeld might have had was that a famous international film diva had lost her way and ended up here—if not for seven-year-old Paul who accompanied her, and who this stranger clearly intended to register that very same day at the Seilersfeld grammar school. And although the fact that she was indeed a mother could have helped to generate feelings of reassurance and tolerance, it was precisely the fact of her motherhood which caused daily-increasing and noticeable disapproval from the village community.

Because she was without a husband.

And so Yvonne Schmidt, on her very first day in Seilersfeld, strutted directly and without deviation into the fantasies of the boys, into the very bloodstreams of the men—and into the bile ducts of the women. Had those women discussed topics other than recipes, celebrities or the peculiar way that Frau So-and-So was dressed at the last church service—for instance their own sex lives (which was unthinkable, of course)—they would surely have noticed that their men had slept with them more frequently than usual in the first days following Yvonne Schmidt's arrival.

But that was not something one talked about.

For Berni Kranz this strange woman was an enchanted being, a goddess. There was something so unreal about her, something ethereal, that he stood frozen at the bus stop when he got off the school bus at midday and saw her coming toward him on the sidewalk. With each of her gentle, almost sashaying steps, her hips swung back and forth, throwing small waves into the shimmering light of the muggy June air, and spreading around her body to create an aura which seemed to make time stand still.

Even the sparrows, flying from treetop to treetop, seemed to be able to poise in mid-air like buzzards, in order to get an undisturbed view of her and drink in her magic, which nature manages to cultivate only at very special moments. As she got closer, Berni could see the spot on her neckline where the top of her bosom appeared—and again, small waves billowed at every step. Like jelly, when one bumped into the table. And when she reached the bus stop, a gracious look issued from her big warm eyes and gentle smile from her promising lips. Then she was already past him, leaving a hint of lavender in her train.

That night he took a long time to get to sleep.

On the following Sunday the pastor had given a sermon from his pulpit on the topic of beauty. Not Yvonne's beauty in particular. God forbid! Just on the subject of beauty in general. That it was, of course, just like everything else on God's green earth, created by our loving Creator and thus a good and divine thing. But then he found an elegant slant on this issue. Because, as with other seductive attractions—for example, power or property—beauty is vulnerable to being abused by the devil to lead the righteous into temptation.

He elaborated on the question of how a believer could recognize whether beauty was being offered to him in a divine form, or whether the diabolical grimace of Satan was hiding behind it. To this end, he read from Matthew, Chapter 7: Ye shall know them by their fruits.

Good trees bear no bad fruit and bad trees bear no good fruit. Verify, when you look upon the face of beauty, what kind of fruits it has exposed, created, or borne. He actually used the term "borne." Are they godly fruits—or such as have arisen from sin? By their fruits ye shall know them, and then judge the beauty at whose face you are looking.

This sermon, thought Berni, presents itself with a certain kind of beauty.

Amen.

Now, while Frau Förster cut his bangs, he kept his eyes closed in order to avoid having any hair fall into them. Thus he was able to listen in—with great interest —as his mother, Frau Förster and Frau Berggruber talked about the new woman in the village. Even though it was clear to him that this could hardly be characterized as a conversation. Rather, it was mutual expressions of outrage.

"Whore!" he suddenly heard his mother say.

"Hilde, the boy!" admonished a shocked Frau Berggruber.

"Oh, don't worry; this young man can certainly hear what his mother thinks about her," she replied and rumpled her son's hair, so that Frau Förster had to create his side-part all over again.

Hilde Kranz was by no means a personable woman, and she fought constantly for her unshakable belief that she was always right. Her hairstyle of grayish-blonde interspersed with reddish streaks might actually be described as a "moptop," except for the fact that, on a woman it was called a bowl cut. The pale, slightly sickly skin of her round and plump face also had reddish streaks. She tried—mostly in vain—to cover these streaks up with too much powder, while she had Frau Förster intentionally insert them in her hair.

Discussions with her were always a little unpleasant, because her lower lip was significantly thicker than her narrow upper lip, which gave her a somewhat uppity appearance. Anyone who did enter into a conversation with her (her husband had not done so for years) always had the feeling that they had to choose their words very carefully; her mouth just naturally expressed such skepticism that one intuitively gave a great deal of thought to the words before uttering them.

This effect was reinforced by two small, venomous eyes that were deeply embedded between her fleshy cheeks, and a thick ridge above, giving her eyebrows the look of frazzled grass atop two sand dunes. In fact, her eyes were so deeply embedded that they were permanently squinty, as though some hidden spirit was ready to spring out at her opponent at any moment if the latter said something wrong.

Nevertheless, this energetic woman was appreciated in the village and was well-liked; she was always to be found at the forefront when it came to organizing school, kindergarten or religious festivals, to which she usually contributed significant amounts of treats from the store. Moreover, she would generally extend credit when the end of the month approached.

Normal conversations with her, concerning the usual banalities of interest to the women of the village, were thoroughly enjoyable and humorous. Often it was Hilde Kranz who was the first source of the local news, such as a pregnancy in town, a pending engagement or the like, which was also a reason that most women were glad to spend their time on a short or long chat with her.

So while casual conversations with her were not unpleasant, and even enjoyable, serious debates were something that one generally sought to avoid. And such was now the case in the room.

Although today words like *hussy, obscene, and half-naked* had been tossed around in Frau Förster's kitchen, the word *whore* was of an altogether different nature, which threatened to transform the current, stimulating conversation into a discussion. Because the shopkeeper made clear with her tone of voice, that she had not used this particular word as a simply disparaging and insulting term, but as a precise designation of "that woman's" profession.

And as far as the other two were concerned, that was going too far, especially since there was no valid evidence underpinning such a claim. In addition, the very idea frightened them. On the one hand, they were concerned about Berni, who was sitting right here and being confronted, probably for the first time in his young life, with the sinful abyss of a natural God-given morality unimaginably abandoned; but there was another fear.

A deeper one.

A fear that threatened them and their world in a very fundamental way. And even if this threat at first appeared quite vague, and could not be immediately justified with hard evidence, the consequences of a genuine, in-the-flesh prostitute living in the village would soon become clear. Even if they banded together, they would not be able to prevent their children from growing up with the knowledge of marketable sex, with all the consequences that would have for their moral development and their views of women. To make matters worse, the unfortunate son of this woman would be significantly compromised in his psychic development, since the epithet *son of a whore* or the equivalent would be certain to be applied to him. In addition, there was the fully-justified assumption that their beloved Seilersfeld would be vilified in the surrounding communities, openly or behind closed doors, as *Harlot Town*. Quite apart from the aspect of constantly increasing numbers of strangers coming to

Seilersfeld to seek out Yvonne Schmidt at her Holzgärtner apartment — some of whom were bound to be shady or even dangerous characters. And the very notion was downright shocking when one realized that the whore would be serving her customers in the evening, while in the next room seven-year-old Paul was trying to sleep.

The biggest threat, however, concerned their own marriages. Yvonne Schmidt was no worn-out, ugly old whore, but rather a young, extremely attractive seductress who was already the subject of much talk by the regulars at the local tavern.

Even if none of the Seilersfeld men should succumb to this temptation, there was still the danger that the weekly card-players or the skittles-players at the Heuslinger Gasthof, for example, would not be able to resist such lewd come-ons.

Why are you grinning?

Have you just come from her place?

The women knew from years of experience that such remarks could quickly generate rumors that had the potential to be repeated and spread more widely.

Of course, that man with the grin on his face would have a verifiable explanation for his state of bliss on hand. He got a raise today, he was soon to be a father, or he had at last been able to purchase the TV that he had saved up for so long. But this "Just come from her place, eh?" teasing would become a habit, perhaps even a standing joke among the half-drunken men at the tavern, and the recipient would not always be able to claim a child on the way or announce that he just got a raise.

If Schmidt remained in the village long enough, even the most credible of men wouldn't be able to prove that they had never had anything to do with her. And this fundamental inability of denial would slowly but surely corrode any sense of trust.

Rumors were allegations that were probably false, but nevertheless possible. Simultaneously accurate and yet not accurate. This ever-increasing uncertainty as to whether something was true or conceivable—or even believable—would insidiously make its way into more and more marriages.

Trying not to speak of it, agreeing to smother the general suspicion in a mutually-agreed silence, would inevitably keep the unutterable alive—for it was precisely the silence that fed and gave weight to that-which-cannot-be-said. And what would ultimately be silenced were precisely those married couples who promised themselves that silence would be their savior. The mere presence of a prostitute in the village would bring about consequences which were of the most perfidious type that a harmonious and hitherto functioning community would have to deal with.

Again, they were not immediately aware of these consequences in all their specific details, but they felt the danger instinctively. And that was certainly the reason that they at first so violently disagreed with Hilde Kranz, even though direct opposition was usually something that one avoided if at all possible — especially if it was expressed vehemently.

But on this day they contradicted her. It simply couldn't be as bad as all that. She was disappointed this time in the expectation that her friends would, as usual, go along with her typically dogmatic vehemence. Hilde Kranz remained calm, first shooing her son from the kitchen chair (around which Birgit Förster then swept up the fallen scraps of another futile yearned-for Beatle haircut), and then sat smugly in his place because she was next in line.

Then she spread the facts out before them.

This Schmidt woman had rented the Holzgärtner apartment, but obviously did not work. She had no job in Seilersfeld, and she hadn't made any effort thus far to find one. She also obviously didn't work outside the village, because she didn't seem to own a car, and she spent all day in the apartment, the only exceptions being her rare visits to the bakery or in Hilde's store. And although she seemed to have no source of income, this Schmidt woman always had an unusually large number of banknotes in her wallet when she opened it at the checkout counter. At the school, she had called herself a *housewife* when asked her profession. So what did she live on? And where was the boy's father? She was surely too young to be a widow. Of course, you could never know for sure. An accident, a terminal illness. Naturally, such a thing is conceivable. But it was not highly likely, right?

Maybe she didn't even know who the father was—given all her "contacts."

Birgit Förster and Ruth Berggruber sighed audibly. Berni however, tried to act as unconcerned as possible, leafing through the pages of the *Passauer Neue Presse*. He was afraid that his mother would send him home at any moment, but she seemed to have forgotten him completely. And then she presented her stunned listeners with a piece of information that only she had known until this moment—with the exception of her husband, from whom she had heard it.

Every evening, Peter Kranz took his van and supplied the surrounding farms, small villages and other isolated areas all those necessities from his shop. He had noticed something which his wife, as soon as she heard it, knew just exactly what was going on.

There were evenings when, just after sunset, he drove out of Seilersfeld and noticed a luxury car—obviously not from the village—parked in front of the Holzgärtner apartment. And when he returned to Seilersfeld after completing his rounds, he saw a single gentleman exit the apartment, climb into the parked car and drive away. The really remarkable thing was that on these evenings there were different men with different cars. Once it was a Mercedes from Munich, another night it was a dark blue Opel Rekord from Augsburg, then there was a black Porsche from Passau.

Birgit Förster and Ruth Berggruber each let out short, frightened sounds, and Hilde Kranz basked for a moment in the glory of having been completely correct.

This afternoon, something had happened in Birgit Förster's kitchen which had never happened before: the hairdresser began working on Hilde Kranz's hair, and all three women kept silent, lost in thought.

They would definitely need to talk with their husbands.

For Berni, it was as though the Queen had been dethroned. He felt disappointed—but also strangely excited at the same time.

2

Gustl and Wilma Holzgärtner's farm was the last group of buildings when one left Seilersfeld to the north. It was on the right-hand side, just before the road made a long curve to the west, approximately a thousand meters after the last residential house. The buildings formed a horseshoe shape, with the open side facing the road. To the east and north stretched pastures and fields.

It was already late. The daylight was giving way to a blurry dark gray, and it would soon be dark.

Michl rumbled into the yard with the new Hatz tractor that his father had bought last year. To his right was the old house with the extension facing the road. The connecting wall of the horseshoe was formed by the long stable, at a right angle from the eastern gable end of the house. Between the stable and the barn on the left side of the horseshoe was a passage to a shed in the back. Michl drove the tractor into the shed, dismounted, turned on the neon lights and closed the heavy overhead door.

The shed was cluttered with pitchforks, rakes, shovels and all the other tools that were needed on a farm. In one corner stood two plows, and in the other a large silver metal locker, the door of which was secured with a simple padlock.

Michl was excited.

His father had sent him after supper to a pasture to repair a section of fence while it was still light out. Although he would normally have been annoyed by such a chore, this time he went readily without grumbling, because this way he wouldn't be back until it was dark. That's why he had secretly taken the key to the padlock on the locker. Now he pulled it from his pocket and opened the locker. The compartments were filled with tools, wires, cans full of nails, screws and other clutter. But his father also kept the binoculars he had brought back from the war here. Michl grabbed them and closed the door. Then he turned off the lights and crept out through the side door.

Looking around, he crossed the short distance to the barn and disappeared into it, finding his way to the stairs in the dark. He climbed carefully up and crawled along the floor to the side of the building facing the yard. There, a small piece of broken board gave a clear view to the outside through a horizontal gap that was about three inches high and three feet wide.

He lay down on his stomach and looked through the gap out to the front of the house and the extension. Only now did he realize what he had not noticed before: a silver NSU Prinz parked in front of the extension. From here he couldn't see the license plate, but he was sure that this car was also from out of town. Like the others, whose owners had visited Yvonne.

She had lived here with little Paul for more than three weeks, in the extension where Grandma and Grandpa used to live.

On the last Thursday in May, the day after a bad storm, a delivery truck had driven into the yard, and two men in gray overalls had carried several suitcases and bags, a chest of drawers, a dressing table with a mirror and a dozen or so large cardboard boxes into the extension. When Michl arrived home on the school bus at noon the next day, this beautiful woman and her little boy were sitting in his kitchen and eating lunch with his parents.

His mother said that Yvonne was something like a distant aunt, but that he didn't need to use the word aunt, he could just call her Yvonne. But he was so intimidated and at the same time fascinated by her, since he had seen her for the first time that day in the kitchen, that he'd addressed her ever since as "Mrs. Yvonne," though she'd already told him a few times that he could omit the "Mrs."

When he noticed after a few days that this distant aunt didn't help in any way around the house, he'd asked his mother about it. I don't need her, she told him. Yvonne pays every month for the extension—and much more than enough, she added. She could put this money to much better use right now than seeking help from an unskilled city girl who would only break her fingers milking the cows.

24

From his position on the barn floor, looking through the opening in the wall, he had a perfect downward view of the apartment's kitchen and parlor. These were the two rooms that faced the yard. Grandma's and Grandpa's bedrooms were in the back. Grandpa's room was now Paul's and Oma's was now the beautiful aunt's bedroom.

He'd love to have a look in there, but even if it had faced the front, this newly-arrived woman always kept the shutters closed, even during the day. His only hope was to see her in the parlor or in the kitchen. Maybe, if he was really lucky, she'd only be wearing her underwear, or even…the very thought made him dizzy.

He lay on his stomach, supporting himself with his elbows, and held the binoculars to his eyes. The parlor window had only curtains that had not yet been drawn. The kitchen window was divided in the middle by a thin rod, from which hung a white lace curtain covering the lower half of the window. From his vantage point, however, Michl could see over it into the kitchen. Both rooms were lit, but there was no one there. Michl could see neither the woman nor her visitor. The only thing he could observe clearly was a man's gray hat on the round table, which occupied the middle of the room, and a dark jacket hanging over the armrest of a chair. For a long while nothing happened, and he had to put the binoculars down several times because his arms got tired of holding them.

Then, suddenly he noticed movement. He immediately brought the binoculars back into position and focused on the parlor. The door to the hallway opened and Yvonne came into the room. Michl's heart beat faster and harder, because she was wearing only a dressing gown. The image in front of him began to tremble—because his hands were doing the same. The gown had slipped slightly from her left shoulder, and Michl could clearly see the narrow white strap of her bra. He was quite excited. A man he did not recognize entered the room after her. He wore suit trousers, a white shirt and a tie. The two of them sat down. The man took the chair where his jacket hung, and Yvonne sat down opposite him. Then the man said something. Yvonne nodded, stood up and walked down the hallway to the kitchen. She filled a glass with water and left the kitchen again.

Michl turned the binoculars back to the parlor. He watched as the man pulled out his wallet and laid some bills on the table and then pocketed his wallet again. Yvonne came back with the water and handed it to the man, who downed it quickly, as if he were really thirsty. Then her eyes fell on the bills. She took the money and put it into one of the pockets of her robe; then she leaned down to the stranger on the chair and gave him a kiss on the forehead. He rose, pulled on his jacket and took his hat from the table. Then he hugged Yvonne briefly and left alone through the front door.

And as he got into his NSU, backed out of the yard and drove away, Yvonne went back into the kitchen, got a large coffee cup from one of the hanging cabinets, tucked the rolled-up wad of cash into it, and put the cup back. From what Michl could see, there was even more money in the cup. Then the kitchen light went out, and shortly afterwards the parlor light as well.

Michl Holzgärtner left his post. At last he had seen something. He had seen Yvonne in her dressing gown, even the strap of her bra. It was a start. He'd definitely be able to score plenty of points with the other boys at school. Maybe they'd even be willing to pay a bit of money if he let them into the barn with him.

No guarantees, of course.

Obviously.

3

Benedict Marquardt had rolled down both windows of his VW Beetle before starting out, and now he enjoyed the warm afternoon air that penetrated the car from both sides of the road, carrying the smell of wheat fields with it. He was on the way back from Passau to Seilersfeld, where he lived in his father's house. The 37-year-old professional journalist worked as editor of *Passauer Neue Presse*, and the dark gray VW was one of the few private cars in Seilersfeld.

Strictly speaking, the car was only partly his, because the publisher had contributed some money for its acquisition. In return he was obligated to use it to travel to all remote assignments. Usually this occurred two or three times a week. He would then write his article on-site, then use the telephone to dictate it to the paper no later than 10:00 p.m., in order that it could appear the next day. The rest of the time he did his routine tasks in his office at the *Passauer*. The paper covered everything that mattered to the residents of Bavaria. Around the office, his department was referred to by his colleagues as "G&S."

That's not for us. Let G&S cover it.

Gossip and Scandal.

Benedict constantly tried not to get upset about this attitude. This formal and official-sounding acronym G&S was naturally used with a degree of condescension that made it difficult for Benedict to keep his composure. It didn't even warrant the term ignorance. As a result, he had now reached the point where he simply resigned himself to it. It wasn't just that the department where he'd worked for many years was ridiculed by everybody that aggravated him, but rather the fact that he was still working at this job after years and had not made it any farther up the ladder. He had often applied for openings in other departments, but had been passed over every time.

Not because he'd be a bad journalist, on the contrary! He had exactly that combination of skills that characterized a good journalist. His research was comprehensive. Moreover, he had a strong sense of perception, and the necessary charm, to elicit from the people involved the nuances, details or hidden relationships of a given situation that could transform a story into a new direction. And besides, he had the talent to write in a gripping and poignant style, such that his articles offered the reader a unique and sometimes even an exciting experience.

It was also not as if these skills marked him as essential for the society pages, simply to keep things on an even keel. A man with his skills would actually be a better fit in a more important department, such as politics—where he wished he was. But the most recent opening in the political department had been filled by a young man, fresh out of journalism school, and with no practical experience. This was an affront, and proved that it was not about his ability, but the idea that

Benedict Marquardt should be deliberately and consistently ignored.

The reason for this seemed to lie in his manner or in his body language. While he came across to the society figures about whom he wrote as gallant, charming and accommodating, and whom he bonded with easily, he was somehow not able to exhibit these characteristics when dealing with his co-workers. This was the result of a relationship—which worked in both directions—because his colleagues (not just those from other departments, but also those from his own) could never deal with him in an unbiased manner.

His habit of either speaking monosyllabically (when the topic was insignificant) or aggressively (when the goal was to achieve or prevent a certain result) lay at the root of it. The upshot was always that managers who had to decide on his application to work in a different department also had to take into consideration the collective displeasure and resistance of the other employees toward Benedict.

This icy relationship was reinforced by the awkward, almost helpless biases that most of them felt in the face of his disability.

Benedict's left arm was shorter than his right. And his left shoulder was narrower than his right, and so his whole posture seemed asymmetrical and crooked. Everyone who met him got the irrational impression that they were in the presence of a man who was deceitful and devious. That was nonsense, of course, because physical deformity had nothing to do with the character of a person — and certainly not in the case of Benedict Marquardt.

In fact, he was loyal, supportive, compassionate and honest — at times even a little too honest in the opinion of some, especially when it came to trying to win an argument. The fact that he shared the same physical disability with Wilhelm II, the last German Kaiser, gained him neither sympathy nor acceptance, but rather numerous nicknames, both at school and now, among his co-workers. They called him *Willi*. In his absence, at home in Seilersfeld and at work, he was the *Kaiser*. Those who wanted to give him a dig greeted him with "Hello, Your Grace," and when he had to make corrections in an employee's article, it was clear, of course, that *His Majesty* knew what was best.

It was Friday, and for once, he had a free weekend before him. Usually, he had to travel on Saturdays and Sundays, as many of the social events on which he reported took place on weekends. The newbie, who had been assigned to the political section instead of Benedict, had to fly the next day to Berlin for an entire week. But it wasn't gloating that Benedict felt, but envy.

For a week, the greenhorn would be the assisting the correspondent in Berlin for the pending visit of the Kennedys to the city. He would see Kennedy and Konrad Adenauer and Willy Brandt. That would have been an assignment which Benedict could have used to distinguish himself for further stories.

Instead, he would be going to Nuremberg on Monday, to report on the first day of the trial against the head of the Nuremberg building department, who had accepted bribes. Then, on Tuesday, there would be a public memorial in Ingolstadt for the seven children who'd been shot by a crazed gunman in a kindergarten exactly half a year ago. At any rate, the Bavarian Prime Minister Alfons Goppel would be participating in this ceremony, and an interview had been set up with him. Goppel would answer the question of how he intended to prevent such shootings in the future. Benedict knew, of course, that it was difficult if not impossible to stop such acts from happening when the perpetrator was an individual who had lived as a normal and well-respected citizen right up to the moment he lost it.

But an interview with the Prime Minister of Bavaria was something, after all. Maybe he could elicit something more than just the conventional answer that the penalties must be increased in order to deter such behavior.

The gunman had been shot dead by the Ingolstadt police at the scene. What good would increased penalties do when being shot by the police was the second most frequent result in such cases—right behind the perpetrator shooting himself? And anyway, a life sentence was the penalty for such shootings. Benedict was looking forward to this interview.

On Friday, he didn't have to drive that far. He would be attending a cattle-show in Landshut. He wasn't at all pleased with that—aside from the fact that it would certainly be boring—but he'd had to swallow this particular bitter pill to land the Goppel interview.

The golden dome of the church tower was the first thing that came into view as the country road ascended the last hill at the south end of the village. He soon passed the first houses, mostly two-storied with yellow painted facades behind fences which meticulously lined the road.

Individual trees, whose trunks were ringed by neatly-laid cobblestones, threw a mosaic of shady patches on the otherwise bright and sun-flecked ground. On a small side-road, some boys drove small wooden wheels with sticks, and in front of the old village well a group of girls with colorful dresses and long braids skipped rope. A gray-brown mongrel dog was dozing on the steps in front of a half-opened door.

Benedict drove his VW Beetle slowly through his home village, which seemed to be completely contented with a warm and satisfying peacefulness. He parked in front of the Peter and Hilde Kranz's grocery store and got out. He wanted to buy cigarettes and a package of salt before he went home, because he'd run out of both. He opened the shop door, and the little bell at the top of the frame tinkled.

Bing-a-ling.

He was greeted by the aroma of freshly-ground coffee, mint, parsley and floor wax, which was permeated by a barrage of different fruity scents, which however did not come from the oranges, bananas and lemons lying in baskets, but from the three women who were chatting excitedly around the counter.

"You can't send your children to fetch eggs or milk, if that's true," said Edith Wagner in an outraged voice.

"There's no way we can allow this. We need to have a talk with Gustl. He has to get rid of her," added Irene Bachleitner all the while tugging nervously on her flowered dress.

"And if he doesn't do it," Edith now turned to Hilde Kranz, who was standing behind the counter, "then your Peter must get eggs and milk from the Stoider farm, and then we'll buy them only from you."

"I've already spoken to the mayor." Now Mechthild Hofreiter—who had a reputation for tackling matters that needed to be tackled—entered the conversation.

"And?"

"And I told him that we don't want someone like that here. Is there no regulation under which she can be gotten out of Seilersfeld? Moral principles, or something of that sort? But he said she's properly registered with the district administration and also presented a legally-binding lease with the Holzgärtners, and thus far there's no evidence for her guilt. She is, after all, a German citizen, and they cannot tell her where to live, or forbid her from living anywhere. I said…but the children! And he said, he understood what I meant…"

"But...?"

"But he could do nothing."

Hilde struck her fist angrily on the counter.

"But that's nonsense," Mechthild continued. "Then I phoned my brother-in-law in Munich. He's a lawyer and said that we can certainly do something. Sepp (Josef "Sepp'" Hirschlsberger, the mayor of the town) could declare the entire village of Seilersfeld a restricted area—or whatever you call it. He can do that, it's an applicable law, my brother-in-law says. And then you can throw her out. And you could also punish her for doing what she's doing in a house where a child is living, namely her own. And then they can take the child away from her, too. But the simplest thing, says my brother-in-law is to talk to Gustl. Tell him that he, as the landlord, would be liable for procurement, which is punishable by at least one month in jail and a fine— he could even lose his rights as a German citizen. We can threaten him with that, and then he'd throw her out on his own, the tramp."

Benedict had remained out of the conversation, leafing through some magazines on a rack off to the side. The ladies' clique hadn't taken any notice of him. He'd already heard about the new woman who'd moved into the Holzgärtner's apartment. He'd not seen her yet because he was usually travelling all week for the newspaper; and he also hardly ever took part in the social life of the village—aside from the occasional card games with Peter Kranz and Hubert Förster and the inevitable festivals.

She was said to be attractive.

Very attractive.

What he had just heard, though, had not pleased him at all. In the past, he'd documented more than once the stories of similar villages whose inhabitants had brought a calamity down on themselves because they couldn't resist spreading tales of intrigue, suspicion and threats, all supposedly to protect the community—be it, as here, the marginalization of an unpopular person, or the expansion of a bypass road through the property of an inhabitant or the demolition of an old house which some residents considered a village eyesore.

In this case, the "creative" Mechthild Hofreiter had offered the others the opportunity to use the heretofore highly-respected Gustl Holzgärtner to get their way in driving the new resident out, by threatening him with a charge of procurement, prison and the loss of his political rights. This was the classic "beginning of the end," as Benedict had learned elsewhere when he investigated the disintegration of hitherto well-functioning and harmonious communities.

Some small trickle began flowing, got steadily wider, broadened into a stream, then picked up speed and began carrying sand and debris with it, which carved furrows into previously solid ground until the foaming spray of envy and resentment transformed itself from a siege mentality and social abortion into a torrent that could not be stopped and threatened to crash down upon Seilersfeld and wash away the solidarity and basic trust of an entire generation. The only thing that would remain would be the hollow facade of respect and mutual trust. Perhaps someone would attempt to apply a new coat of paint, but it would be in vain.

Benedict was about to turn his attention to the women and say something when a bright bing-a-ling suddenly altered the situation. The subject of the conversation herself entered the shop. Yvonne Schmidt wore a long brown dress, fitted with a wide, beige leather belt. In spite of the hot weather outside, it was markedly cool in the shop.

Now it became oppressively cold.

Where just moments ago there had been a loud and agitated clamor, it was suddenly deathly still, as though a heavy snowfall in the middle of June had covered the bustling village with a heavy cloak of total paralysis and silence.

"Good afternoon," Yvonne said a bit timidly, having noticed the sudden silence. Her voice had a clear and bright inflection, and Benedict Marquardt understood immediately why the Mechthilds and Hildes of the village were trying so hard to hide their own shortcomings.

Hilde Kranz broke the silence in a clearly hostile tone of voice.

"Yes…?"

"Is it already my turn?" she asked in her melodious voice.

"Yes, it's your turn!" came the brisk reply.

Yvonne took a few tentative steps past the three other customers and stepped up to the counter—behind which the owner glared with folded arms, narrowed eyes and a protruding lower lip—and asked for a pound of ground coffee, a package of egg noodles and two bottles of orange soda.

"Coffee, noodles and soda are sold out," came the reply. The young woman in the brown dress seemed not to have immediately understood this response, and pointed to the packages of coffee that were clearly visible on the shelf behind Hilde's back.

"But..."

"Those are already sold."

Yvonne Schmidt looked at the woman, bewildered. Her eyes betrayed a surprised, almost amused disbelief combined with a desperate attempt on her part to grasp the meaning of something that could only be understood if she ignored the words *coffee, noodles* and *soda* in Hilde's reply. Only then did her face reveal that she understood the true meaning behind Hilde's statement. Yvonne turned around slowly and looked into the eyes of the other three women, one after the other, and getting the same open rejection from each of them. Then she wordlessly turned on her heel and walked out of the shop to the accompaniment of a bright bing-a-ling.

"What was that?" Now Benedict spoke up and pushed past Edith, Mechthild and Irene to the counter.

"She can go to hell. She's not getting anything more from me," said Hilde Kranz in a cool and determined manner.

"Why? What did she do?"

"Now listen up, Willi; what will become of our beautiful village if a hooker is living here and serves her clients here?"

"What do you mean, a hooker?"

And then Hilde Kranz presented to him all the facts that she had already laid out while getting her hair done in Birgit Förster's kitchen, and with which she had already convinced all the others that Yvonne Schmidt was a prostitute. Benedict listened to it all quietly. Then he turned to the other three, as he pointed to Hilde with his outstretched healthy arm.

"*This* is nonsense, ladies. This doesn't prove anything. Before you disrespect old Gustl—or do anything else of the kind, you need irrefutable proof that Frau Schmidt is a prostitute. And *that*..." He waved with his forefinger under Hilde double chin indignantly, "is not proof! It's simply rash fantasies!"

"We'll find proof, you can count on it," snapped Mechthild, and he quickly realized that their original desire to never have a whore in the village had mutated, now that Yvonne Schmidt was here, into having one at all costs. He turned back to the counter and faced Hilde Kranz.

"I'd like a pack of Lucky Strikes, salt, a pound of ground coffee, a package of egg noodles and two bottles of orange soda."

She turned out of habit to the shelf behind her and reached for the cigarettes, then suddenly stopped. Then she spun around, as if stung by a tarantula, leaned on the counter with tightly clenched fists and stared at the man in front of her with a hateful glare. She searched for words, but the lips of her open mouth only trembled.

"I'd like a pack of Lucky Strikes, salt, a pound of ground coffee, a package of egg noodles and two bottles of orange soda," he repeated, looking her confidently in the eye without flinching.

"Or could it be that a respected editor of the *Passauer Neue Presse*, who has never before published anything about his own village—or about certain families who live there—is no longer able to be served here?"

4

Anyone who saw Yvonne for the first time and didn't know her would automatically think of her as one of those modern women, the kind who were never at a loss for words. A harbinger of a revolutionary period that was inevitably on its way.

In fact, the facts were exactly opposite.

She had always felt that her life had been something like a game of soccer—but without rules or referees. And she was the ball, being kicked around at random, with no control, and no way to influence the outcome of the game in any way.

And she was at the end of her wits.

Her reserves, if indeed she had ever had any, had been completely consumed. She had grown up as the youngest of five children, and what was more, had the misfortune to be born a girl. Actually, that could have been an advantage, if only her father had been one who was strict with his sons, but indulgent with his little daughter. But, regrettably, it was not so. In her family it was rather the reverse. She couldn't seem to do anything right. Even sunny and playful days were always obscured by a shadow cast by the knowledge of both the children and their mother that the day would end with their father's return from the factory or— worse—from the pub.

What followed was not determined by the quality of the evening meal, the immaculate state of the children's rooms or of the type of flowers in the vase on the dining-room table in the room, but only his mood, which he brought with him from his day at the factory or from the number of drinks he'd consumed at the pub.

The best time of her life was when she was still in school. Unlike most students, she and her brothers enjoyed going to school, because they didn't have to be at home. At home, their mother ruled in her husband's absence with comparable severity and cruelty. Either she was completely overwhelmed with five children and a wife-beating husband, or she was compensating for her humiliating inferiority with her own tyrannical power that she believed she had over the children.

In any case, because they felt comfortable at school, the siblings brought home above-average marks. Their grades were much better than their father's had ever been, and unlike him, they were all able to take the school-leaving examination. Except for Yvonne.

While their father threatened to beat his sons if they even suggested that they didn't want to sit for it, he literally did beat Yvonne for merely saying that she wanted to do the same. Who did she think she was, he asked her; who put such ideas into her head? It was one thing if the boys lived off the family for a couple of years; after all, they would eventually amount to something. But she should learn a thing or two about running a home and family, something that's proper for a woman.

And then, after her schooling was over, he led her instead to the altar, where he handed her over to Horst Schmidt, a fellow factory worker.

With the words: "Now she belongs to you."

Horst was twelve years older than she. They met when her father brought him home one evening, along with several of his other co-workers, so that they, armed with a case of beer, could listen to the final game of the German Football Championship on the radio. Horst was nice. Again and again he broke away from the others and the broadcast under some pretext to come into the kitchen, where she was sitting. She was making canapés and cheese snacks for the men and placing empty beer bottles back in the crate and full ones in the refrigerator. He flirted with her, complimented her and impressed her in many ways. Not only did he seem to care more for her than for his friends or the football game, he even helped her with the sandwiches. He wooed her with a charm which was seductively restrained and natural—and he looked damn good as well.

Horst was tall and strong, he wore his black hair slicked straight back raffishly, and it had a noble, soft shine from the pomade with which he tamed it. Together with the neat mustache, which consisted of two separate thin strokes, he reminded her of a young Errol Flynn. What attracted her more than anything, though, were his eyes, in which a fire was burning, in which she saw mirrored her own longing, the promise of passion and adventure, the promise of a life of her own, the prospect of escape. To get out of the cramped and dismaying storage closet that her parents had made of her life.

Her mother had always been against the relationship with Horst, because Yvonne's marriage would leave her at home alone with her husband. But Yvonne did not feel sorry for her in the least: her mother had too often denied her the solidarity, the protection and warmth and security that Yvonne needed. Her father, on the other hand, seemed anxious to get rid of her, because he actively encouraged the relationship with Horst. And even if he did it only to get her out of the house, it was the first and only time that Yvonne felt grateful to him: when he agreed to Horst's request for her hand while aggressively cutting off his wife's tentative "but…" in a manner which left no doubt who was the authority here.

Horst took her dancing or to the movies, and she enjoyed her newfound freedom on the one hand, and on the other hand the apparent pride that he—twelve years her senior—exhibited when he showed up somewhere with her.

Of course, she could not stay overnight with him before the wedding; that would have been unthinkable in spite of her father's enthusiasm for the relationship. But they managed to find opportunities when they were together. They married when Yvonne was 21, and there followed the long-awaited move into his apartment.

But what followed had finally eliminated her strength, self-assertion and self-confidence that she otherwise would have employed against Hilde Kranz. All the charm, the easy-going manner, the courtesy, the attentiveness and the sense of humor that Horst had displayed—and which he continued to show to others —suddenly disappeared as soon as they were married and Yvonne moved in with him. The fire in his eye that had promised passion and a zest for life, turned into a nervous flicker of an insecure soul, hiding behind imperiousness, antagonism and jealousy.

Up to now, Yvonne had lived in what amounted to a storage closet; now she was confined to a tool shed, from which she was only released to go to work. She didn't know how he managed it, but he would occasionally slip away from the factory in the afternoon and be waiting for her at four o'clock, in order to check whether she came straight home from work.

Two years later, Paul came into the world, and she took a three-year maternity break, during which she virtually could not leave the house without Horst. It was only when Paul entered kindergarten that she was allowed to resume working. When she fell ill and could not go to work, a concerned colleague had come to check on her. And though Yvonne became visibly more nervous as the day went on, she did not manage to get her colleague to leave before Horst arrived home shortly after six.

As long as the woman was present, he behaved in his usual charming and friendly manner. But after she left, he beat her.

And between each blow, senseless interrogation.

What did you tell her?

Did you tell her I was an asshole?

Were you whining and complaining?

Whack!

Or was she sent by another guy?

Whack!

What's his name?

Who is it?

Who did you meet?

Whack! Whack!

While one could simply accept a rainstorm or a severe winter as something immutable that would eventually pass, Yvonne looked upon the life that she had ended up in as something equally immutable—except that there was no hope that it would pass.

She usually managed to arrange things so that Horst had no reason for his attacks of jealousy. And over the course of the marriage, the situation improved.

With one exception.

That was the albeit brief affair with her boss, in which she had become involved out of a desperate desire for love and attention, for understanding and a sense of security. Horst had not learned of this affair either while it was going on nor afterwards. Nevertheless, it was the reason for the catastrophe that would result years later, and for which she was now stranded on a dead-end road in this one-horse town. A virtual blizzard of hostility—which she could no longer bear—then erupted around Yvonne and lasted for weeks and months, from neighbors, from strangers, even from those few friends who Horst and she had, but also from her former colleagues.

The exclusion and social isolation that she had to suffer were as full and complete as her sense of guilt she felt over her affair. But she deserved every bit of it. She had brought it on herself, and she could not forgive herself.

So why should anyone else forgive her?

She wouldn't be able to carry this burden on her already weakened shoulders for very long. She barricaded herself in the apartment for weeks, to the point where she was no longer even startled by the sound of the balloons filled with red paint bursting on her windowpanes. And she would surely have put an end to her bungled life if it were not for Paul, and if her eldest brother had not been there for her.

He had saved her.

He came and ignited a small glimmer of hope in her murky swamp of guilt, despair and resignation when he told her that his wife's sister was married to a man whose sister owned a farm somewhere in Lower Bavaria. It was in a small village, in the middle of nowhere, so there was no chance that anybody would know her; and what was more, there was an outbuilding on this farm, a fully-furnished apartment that had been empty for quite a while.

Here she could start over again. Incognito.

She had cautiously begun to feel reasonably good, especially since, after meeting Wilma and Gustl Holzgärtner, she had felt for first time in what seemed an eternity friendliness and welcome. They, their son Michl, and the two workers, had taken Paul by the hand and showed him around the farm. They had taught him how to feed the chickens and gather the eggs in the morning. They had shown him the horses, pigs and cows, and how you could build a haystack in the barn and play in it. Since arriving here, she saw Paul thriving. What had once been a deeply intimidated boy had become a cheerful young man. Yvonne hoped that this would help him to forget the trauma of the past.

But the stone wall of rejection that she had just encountered in the village grocery store had brought back the feelings of grief, of unpleasant memories and of quiet desperation; a lump formed in her throat, making it not only impossible for her to utter a single word, but forcing her to leave the shop immediately to avoid bursting into tears in front of these women. She strode briskly out of the center of the village, but her legs soon gave out and she stumbled slightly on her high-heels to a bench in front of the statue of Mary at the edge of the village. She sat down and fell into tearless, dry sobbing consisting only of a gurgling deep in her throat.

She did not understand it.

It could not possibly start again. It drove her into a dark valley of complete solitude, forsaken by God and Man alike.

She felt abandoned, discarded as something worthless.

A dark gray VW Beetle sped past her and braked about a hundred meters down the road. Then it backed up a bit and parked at the edge of the road. Yvonne sniffled and sat up straight. A man she did not know — but somehow looked familiar — got out of the car. Then she remembered: she thought she'd seen him in the store, at the magazine rack. He'd been there, along with the others.

The man paused for a moment beside his Beetle and looked over at her. Somehow, it seemed to her, his posture was wrong. She couldn't tell the reason right away, but he didn't give the impression of an upright, straightforward person. Then he walked toward her and took a seat beside her on the bench.

"I'm Benedict, Benedict Marquardt. I was in the shop a few minutes ago when you came in. Do you remember?"

Yvonne looked down at the sidewalk and nodded shyly.

"Whether you believe me or not, I didn't think it was right how they treated you," he continued.

"I took the liberty, therefore, of buying a pound of coffee, egg noodles and two bottles of orange soda for you."

Yvonne straightened, turned to him and looked into his eyes. Now he was the one who could not resist the look of this incredibly beautiful—and desperate—woman, so he simply nodded his head towards his car.

"They're in the car, and if you don't mind, I'll drive you, the coffee, the noodles and the soda to the farm."

5

Yvonne took the boiling water off the stove and poured it through the filter. Then she took the full pot of coffee back into the living room, filling the air with its aroma. Benedict sat at the table and looked around the room. He saw a few of his hostess' personal belongings. The good Sunday table-service behind the glass doors of the buffet was from the estate of the elder Holzgärtners, as was the embroidered tablecloth and the V-shaped newspaper rack next to the wing chair.

"Do you want milk or sugar?" asked Yvonne, as she poured the steaming coffee in his cup.

"Just milk, thank you," he said. She then filled her cup and sat at the table, opposite him. Paul stayed in Wilma's kitchen, where he was eyeing the tiny kitten that Mimi the house cat had just given birth to. They sipped circumspectly from their cups, glanced occasionally at each other, waiting for the opportunity to gingerly broach the subject that was on both of their minds. The journalist then simply skipped over that barrier.

"Where are you from, and what brought you here to Seilersfeld?" he asked her, breaking the silence. His success as a reporter was due in large part to the quality of his voice when he asked questions. It encompassed gentleness and a kind of understanding empathy. Yvonne gazed into her coffee shyly. Then she said quietly:

"I wonder, rather, what I'll do, now that I'm no longer allowed to buy anything here," cleverly avoiding his question.

Benedict was of course a man like any other, and he immediately felt the impulse to help her with this problem. But he was experienced enough to know he'd have to use his proposed solution to bring the discussion back to his question.

"It's possible that Wilma will need to bring you everything you need. But if I understood the women in the store properly, they don't want to buy eggs or milk from her as long as you live here. And it may be that the Holzgärtners themselves won't be able to buy anything here in town. They'll be forced to terminate their lease with you in order to get you out of here."

Yvonne felt immediately that same lump in her throat, stifling any attempt at an answer. She buried her face in her hands. How could this be? How could the people of Seilersfeld know anything about her? Had the Holzgärtners said something? She couldn't imagine that, as she considered both of them completely trustworthy. And their son Michl knew nothing. It was bad enough that certain people apparently hated her, but she certainly didn't want her caring landlords drawn into it.

She felt her hands being grasped gently but firmly by two masculine hands, one of them slightly larger and stronger than the other. They pulled her hands away from her face and placed them gently on the table, then carefully covered hers. Benedict's hands felt warm and tender, like the hands of a man who has never had to do manual labor. She wondered how he earned his living. Yvonne couldn't look him in the eyes or at his dissimilar hands. Then Benedict spoke to her again. His tone was soft and quiet, as if he were speaking to a child.

"The women in the store think that you..." he paused briefly, "are a prostitute."

Yvonne lifted her head abruptly and looked him directly in his face. She smiled, and her eyes suddenly became bright and clear. It was as if a light had gone on inside her head, illuminating the lonely and mysterious darkness that had taken root there.

"What? Really?" She gasped, and her voice skipped a beat, as if he had brought her very good news.

Benedict was visibly surprised by this reaction; he had expected her to express shame or indignation, depending on whether she really was a prostitute or not. But he had not reckoned with joy, which she clearly seemed to feel. He pulled his hands away from hers and put them in his lap, so that Yvonne could no longer see them.

"That seems to amuse you," he said, a little dismayed.

"Yes, that is, I mean, naturally, no. But it relieves me somehow," she responded, "because that can be easily straightened out. I'm not a prostitute."

Benedict told her about the observations that Peter Kranz had made while making his evening deliveries, and that, for Hilde Kranz and her companions, given these various male visitors, together with the fact that she had no other sources of income and lived without a husband, the obvious assumption was that she supported herself from those male visitors.

"That's true!" Yvonne now admitted to his complete confusion. "My entire livelihood is financed by these men," she said, clearly amused, and poured her visitor another cup of coffee.

"They're my brothers, and they share the expenses of Paul and me until I can work again myself. They help us so that we can find peace of mind and settle down somewhere."

Then she got up, leaned over the table and took his hands, which were folded on his legs, and put them back on the table. Now it was she who put her hands protectively on top of his.

"You don't need to hide, Benedict Marquardt. You are a good man, and I am infinitely grateful to you for what you've done today. You've given me hope. I was completely desperate at first, I felt incredibly lonely, finding out that even here I was considered an undesirable outcast. You don't know what I've been through. But then you came. You are to me like that angel from the Bible. I don't know the Bible that well, but there was one who said, "Do not be afraid," and in principle you have done exactly that for me. You said I had been treated badly; you were there and did not immediately condemn me. You followed me and showed me that you are not one of those. With all this you have told me, "Do not be afraid." You can't imagine how much better I feel and what that means to me."

Benedict felt the woman's warm and soft hands on the back of his, and it felt good. A gentle touch of a woman was something that he'd never known. His disability, and thus his appearance, had so far prevented women from getting any closer than a professional level with him. He felt a strong urge to turn his hands over and take hold of hers. But he controlled himself. That was certainly inappropriate and could be easily misunderstood. Instead, he pulled them, reluctantly, out from under her hands, taking hold of his coffee cup, and once again entering neutral territory. In any case, this brief, intimate situation neither obscured the fact that they were strangers, nor had it satisfied his natural curiosity.

"When I hear you talk like that, I get the feeling that you were running away from something."

He sipped casually at his cup.

Yvonne leaned back again.

"Your brothers are hiding you here, is that right?" he added. "From whom?" he pressed. "Your husband?"

Yvonne got up and began putting the coffee pot, the sugar jar, the jug of milk and her own, still half-full cup on the tray and answered in an audibly cool tone:

"I'm very grateful for all of your help, but with all due respect, I don't know how that concerns you. I don't want to talk about it."

Then she took his cup, put it on the tray, which she carried into the kitchen. That clearly meant that it was time to leave.

Benedict stood up and followed her, then stood in the doorway to the kitchen. His voice again had that pleasant soothing tone that had caught her attention at the beginning. He spoke while she put the dishes in the sink and the milk in the refrigerator.

"I think it's time for me to go home. My father will have already eaten alone. I'd like to help you when you need it. If Hilde Kranz really refuses to sell Wilma anything, you can come to me. I'll bring you what you need from Passau. I work there. If I'm not at home, you can give your shopping list to my father. He's retired and almost always at home. He'll know. We live in the house with the dark green balustrade at the end of Ludwigstraße. You can't miss it. Have a nice weekend, and thanks for the coffee."

"What do you do in Passau?" she asked as she followed him to the door.

"I'm a journalist with the *Passauer*."

A horrified sound escaped from her.

Her voice almost cracked.

"You're a reporter?"

Benedict opened the door and turned back to her.

"A journalist, yes."

Yvonne held the door firmly with one hand and pushed Benedict out with the other.

"So that's it," she shouted angrily, "the great selfless knight in shining armor? You shameless reporters. Leave me alone!"

Then she slammed the door in his face.

Wilma Holzgärtner heard the shouting and stepped out her kitchen into the yard.

"Willi? What are you doing here? What's going on?"

Benedict "Willi" Marquardt explained to her what had happened. He told her of the suspicions of the women in the shop, that Yvonne couldn't buy anything there, and that he had then made the purchase for her. He told her of Yvonne's violent reaction when she learned who he was. His account was accompanied by a look that reflected his truly shocked confusion. He did not mention Mechthild Hofreiter's suggestion to threaten the Holzgärtners with a criminal complaint for procuring. It would surely have the same destructive effect on the townsfolk, so he remained silent on this point. He still hoped to be able to prevent this or similar consequences.

"Oh, the poor thing," said the farmer's wife and put her hand on his good shoulder.

"That was surely just an overreaction. It has nothing to do with you, because you can't do anything about it. She came here looking for peace and quiet, and probably now thinks it's "your kind" that tracked her down. Go home, Willi, I'll talk with her."

Benedict spread his arms in a gesture that indicated that he simply didn't quite understand what was going on.

"Can someone explain to me what this is all about? What exactly is wrong with her?"

"I'm sorry, but I promised not to say anything—and you know me, I won't say anything," Wilma said, and made a gesture as if zipping her lips.

6

Two days later, on Sunday afternoon, a day of bright blue sky and comfortably warm temperature, Yvonne walked down the road into Seilersfeld, then right through the village to Ludwigstraße. The area was quiet and peaceful, nestled between golden-yellow fields, abuzz and whirring, at whose edges the summery green of the forest began.

Yvonne looked for the house with the dark green balustrade that Benedict had described to her—and where he lived with his father. Paul trotted along beside her on her right. In her left hand she held a tote bag containing an apple pie that Paul and she had baked the day before. Before she left home, she gave some thought to the possibility of encountering other villagers on the way, and how she planned to react to any insults or hostile behavior with her small son at her side. But nothing of the sort happened. Although they saw some married couples who were also taking advantage of the beautiful day for a walk in the sun, they crossed over to the other side of the road as soon as they spotted her.

Just minutes after Yvonne had so rudely expelled Benedict from her doorstep the day before yesterday, there had come a knock on her window. It was Wilma. As soon as Paul was in bed, the two women sat together and discussed the situation well into the night. Wilma was able to convince Yvonne that the gossip about her would soon subside, as long as she consistently ignored it, and that she also had nothing to fear from Benedict. The fact that he was a journalist with the *Passauer Neue Presse*, was just a coincidence. He was certainly not one of those who were just trying to locate her. He had just wanted to help her. She explained that she had always called him Willi or Kaiser, and told Yvonne the origin of this nickname. Just like the last German emperor, Benedict had been delivered via a breech birth, which also involved complications, especially since it did not take place in a hospital, but at home. Wilma pointed out that, because there was no doctor present, but only a midwife, both mother and child were lucky to have survived the procedure. But it also led to the same brachial plexus palsy as with Wilhelm II, so Benedict's left arm was stunted and remained shorter than the right. But even so, he was luckier than his prominent fellow sufferer. While the emperor's disability was also marked by greatly reduced mobility of the arm, Benedict's maneuverability was nearly unlimited. It was just slightly shorter than the right, and his shoulder was narrower.

Yvonne had listened to the story attentively, and she was soon sorry that she had treated him in that way. Not because he was disabled—that had not bothered her—but because as Wilma's portrayal made increasingly clear, Benedict was equipped with such a strong and self-confident personality. Perhaps his parents had deliberately raised him with an emphasis on stability and fortitude, or maybe the constant teasing he had endured during his childhood and adolescence had bolstered his character, rather than undermining it.

Whatever his past, Wilma said, the fact was that Benedict was now more or less an outsider in Seilersfeld—though a widely respected and secretly-admired outsider. People got upset when he expressed a different opinion than the majority at a community meeting. And he tended to express himself in somewhat cynical or caustic terms, snappy, and there were certainly a number of folks that were uncomfortable with his habit of pointing out their faintheartedness and indecision. Nevertheless, it happened more than once that he was able to convincingly characterize the inconsistency or the futility of a community plan such that, one by one, the formerly vehement proponents buckled and took his side. The ease with which this man, in spite of his odd physical appearance, knew how to express a dissenting individual opinion to the public, coupled with his unwavering ability to do so with a disarming logic that could lead others to the blurred and vague edges of their own convictions prevented Benedict Marquardt from having many friends—or being closely involved in community life—in Seilersfeld. Often he was the last to be informed of relevant facts. Only with Peter Kranz and the district commissioner Hubert Förster did he have something like a friendship, which had originated at the regular skittles games.

On the other hand it was not uncommon that he was the one who was asked for advice—usually under some pretext or other—when someone needed a reliable and well-founded objective opinion. The relationship of Seilersfeld to its disabled citizen was ambiguous. But while many secretly admired Benedict's inner strength, his analytical skills and his steadfastness, he was also a regular topic at every social get-together because of his reputation as an overly-judgmental dissenter and maverick.

It didn't seem to bother him.

What Yvonne heard made her curious. She was fascinated by this quiet, serene type of personal autonomy described by Wilma when she was speaking of the man who had just told her that she had been mistreated in his eyes. Wilma's words painted the image of a man who had developed a unique inner strength despite (or because of?) his physical disability. She had till now experienced a very different type of masculine strength.

Even as the farmer's wife described Benedict, Yvonne suddenly realized that masculine strength was only what she'd been led to believe. A mask. A strident, roaring mask, made of simple brutality, behind which only uncertainty and fear—but not a trace of serenity—lay hidden.

That fear was that others might see one's actual internal weakness or the inability to grasp the complexity of life. Perhaps it was not even the fear that others saw this, but rather the fear of seeing for one's self. The *angst* of one day looking into the mirror and not being able to see the man one wished to see, but only the true weakling.

After Wilma's portrayal Yvonne had the feeling of having discovered something new, something which at first did not seem to fit into her image of the world. It was the quiet, easy-going independence that Benedict exhibited. What made this discovery extraordinary was not that a strong personality was possible with—or in spite of—a certain serenity. No, the special thing was that it was precisely this serenity that led to personal strength. True strength was only possible through inner serenity.

This new reversal of her world-view, which turned all her previous experience on its head, consumed her thoughts all the next day. On Saturday, when Paul was not exploring the farm, romping around in the hay or playing with the kittens, they played board games, drew pictures or built mighty castles of wooden building blocks while lying on the floor. Still, she was preoccupied, which prevented her from giving her young son the loving attention which she herself had never experienced.

In answer to his questions—mingled with his attempts to handle all the toys spread across the room:

When would school begin? Did she want to see the kittens? Is Papa coming, and when?—she could only reply absentmindedly.

I'm sorry?

School will start when the summer holiday ends, in a while; of course I'd like to see the kittens, what are their names? I already explained to you that Papa left us, and he won't be coming back to see us.

That last answer didn't seem to disturb the boy. On the contrary. Maybe he repeatedly asked just to be really sure. He didn't understand why his father had left, or where he had gone. His mother had not told him, and he never asked. He only seemed to want to hear that he wouldn't be coming back.

In the intervening moments, or when Paul was out of the house, Yvonne gazed over the towers of the wooden castle and saw a cumbersome panorama of rustic, peasant humbleness. A massive, high buffet, whose blue-painted wood had cracked in some places, and the old Sunday table-service still waiting patiently behind the glass doors.

A conservative dark sideboard, whose locks were plated with brass and held spotted, discolored keys with ornate cloverleaf handles.

An old wing chair, threadbare in many places, on whose arms small doilies covered the worst of the many stains. And on the wall hung a framed copy of an oil painting of grazing horses.

All in all, it was an inherited lifestyle that was clearly rich in work and poor in luxury. Nothing in this apartment where she now lived was modern.

The beds with their wooden frames, the much-used furniture, the worn-down carpets and rugs and the crumbling linoleum in the kitchen: nothing was up-to-date.

Water was pumped by hand in the kitchen. A toilet and a warm shower connected to the water system only existed in the main house — and both of them were shared with the residents of the apartment. In the bathroom a gray zinc tub with four curved feet stood on a specially-built platform; you could fill it with buckets of warm water from the kitchen and after bathing, drain the water through a pipe that led through the wall to the outside.

Yvonne had been pleased by this museum-like ambience when she had first arrived here. Not because of its antique atmosphere, but because her surroundings confirmed her sense that, from now on, she was committed to a whole new life. A quiet, natural existence, frugal, governed by nature and the seasons, subject to them and at the same time conforming to them.

Calm.

Enduring by a natural and implicit respect for man and beast, for the necessary work, and for the nature and needs of one's partners and other family members. What had been to her, in the midst of this furnished repository, little more than a vague feeling had now become apparent from Wilma's description of a particularly independent person, which was slowly turning into a strong and tangible longing. The longing for one's own natural way of life, the desire to recognize and feel entitled to one's own ideas of a fulfilled, meaningful and peaceful life.

To recognize oneself as entitled.

Wilma's characterization of Benedict's inner independence formed in her a picture of how everything might have been. As she herself might have been. She fell in love with this idea, it was invigorating.

On this particular Saturday, between all the dice-throwing, between the yellow crayons for the sun and the blue ones for the sky, the different building blocks for the knights' chambers, she let herself be carried away by these thoughts. She let herself drift off into a world where knights were chivalrous, where one's own cozy home was bathed in the light of a yellow sun under blue sky on a green meadow, a world in which people weren't ejected from their homes. And in this world, in these pictures, on this Saturday, a face appeared repeatedly. A friendly face with virtuous, honest eyes. A face that sat calmly and composedly on two unequal but broad shoulders.

The life, through which she had until now only shuffled from one place to the next, seemed to her this time—perhaps even intentionally—to have been moved into exactly the right place.

As Paul took his one-hour midday nap, Yvonne lounged in the threadbare armchair, letting one leg dangle over the armrest, and allowed herself to daydream a little. She was almost 30 and still did not feel like a grown and complete woman. She had never been allowed to feel so—let alone become one. In her wing chair, she now allowed herself the privilege.

She imagined how her life would have turned out if Horst had not behaved the way he had. If he had been as he had at first seemed to be. If he had been like…like Benedict Marquardt.

Her feelings varied with the pictures that arose in her mind's eye. On an imaginary walk in the woods, she felt accepted. Her longing for affection gave her free rein to lay her head on his chest and feel his arm pressing her toward him. In the village store she enjoyed her unprecedented pride and her new Benedict-like independence when she cut Hilde Kranz off short. The first time around in her imagination, she was accompanied by him—her man. When she repeated the fantasy, she stood alone in front of Hilde.

And when she imagined dressing up the apartment (some imaginary apartment), she saw herself lighting a candle on the table and preparing a special dinner that would please him when he came home from work. Then she truly began to love the unfulfilled longing that had been hidden in her heart.

But just before his key turned in the door, the film suddenly stopped. While most of the pictures in her mind were easy to imagine, she now realized that she had no idea what it was like to look forward to the return of her man, not with fear but with joyful anticipation. To see love rather than control in his eyes. To be taken affectionately in his arms rather than to have her own arms twisted. To be greeted with warm, romantic words rather than accusatory and threatening questions.

She cleared her head and went back to the lovely hike through the woods, strolling hand-in-hand to the movies, or walking, proudly, with her head held high through the town. Only the longing and pleasant anticipation of his nightly homecoming would somehow not succeed. She always recognized the smiling and friendly face as that of Benedict, but just before he reached her and could embrace her, Horst's visage pushed through Benedict cheeks, and the bold, wide-open eyes were flickering and exhausted. Sometimes Horst even had the meager yellow strands of hair, combed sideways over his forehead, just like her own father's.

She gave up on the image.

She took her leg off the armrest. Then an inescapable doubt set in. Such a fundamentally independent man, intelligent, educated and self-confident, a man such as Benedict Marquardt, would not know how to deal with her. Such men were comfortable only with partners like themselves: intelligent, educated, independent and self-confident. Women with whom they could discuss, argue, plan on the same level, and with whom they would make up a strong team to face the world. She sighed. Dreams were just that—dreams, she scolded herself.

No, this man had indeed been nice to her; he had taken her side and, what's more, he had been courteous enough to accept her invitation to share the coffee that he'd brought her. But she could hardly expect more than courtesy from him. Once he got to know her better, he would look down on her. And even the courtesy that he had shown her would surely turn into contempt. Especially, when he discovered who she really was. What she had done.

In addition, they had no contact. Aside from her landlords, Yvonne had no contacts in the village, and she wasn't looking for any. She preferred to remain invisible. Hopefully, Wilma was right, and the gossip about her, and the unwelcome attention, would fade away soon. They should just leave her alone.

Yvonne stood up, turned around and looked at the picture of grazing horses on the wall. In the past few weeks it had often given her a sense of tranquility and solace. Two reddish brown Arabian horses—a mare and a stallion—grazed before a background of snow-covered mountains. While the mare was grazing, the stallion laid his head on her flank.

Was there a chance that they would see each other again? She would so like to talk with him, she had a thousand questions. She thought of the tender warmth that had emanated from his hands when he had laid his hands on hers. But she also remembered the shocked look on his face when she'd pushed him out the door. And then she had an idea, one that took all her courage to muster. When an hour had elapsed, she woke her son with the words "Let's bake a pie. We're going to visit someone tomorrow."

They had found the house.

Its facade was painted yellow, like most of the houses in Seilersfeld. The second floor had a wrap-around balcony, which was framed by a dark green balustrade of conical stone struts. In front of the windows with their open shutters hung flower boxes with blooms in every color of the rainbow. Two steps led up to the front door. Yvonne and Paul stood on the upper step. It was the moment that had played itself out in her head repeatedly in the past 24 hours. She had to ring the bell.

"Who are we visiting?" Paul had asked when he'd finally woken from his nap.

"A nice man who helped me by driving me home with things I'd bought in town so I didn't have to walk. I'd like to thank him, and that's why we're baking a delicious apple pie for him. Of course, you'll get a piece of it."

She rang the doorbell.

It took a while, an eternity, it seemed to her, until the door opened. Before them stood a gray-haired man she estimated to be in his mid to late sixties. She immediately noticed the similarity to Benedict. This must be his father. The same kind eyes and the same youthful face—despite the wrinkles.

It took him a moment, however, to realize that this beautiful stranger standing before him must be the one his son had described to him. Beni had certainly not exaggerated. And then, with the same matter-of-factness as his son, he voiced just what he was thinking before Yvonne was even able to introduce herself and Paul and their reason for their visit.

"You're even more beautiful than Beni described you, if you don't mind my saying so."

Yvonne did not know what to say, so surprised was she. On the one hand, because this older man had known immediately who she was; on the other hand because of his outspokenness and, most of all, deep inside her, what Benedict had said about her.

That she was beautiful.

Before she could react, Benedict's father opened the door fully, gesturing with his outstretched arm and inviting them in. The narrow hallway was darker than one would expect. They followed him into the living room, which was located right behind it. Along the way, he called up the staircase that a visitor was here. The living room, however, was spacious and bright. One corner was dominated by a sofa and two armchairs around a low kidney-shaped table, and in the opposite corner was a table with a corner bench and two matching chairs. Their backs were decorated and had heart-shaped cut-outs in the middle. On both the bench and the chairs were patterned cushions.

"Frau Schmidt? What a surprise!"

Yvonne and Paul turned.

And although Yvonne had prepared her son for Benedict's appearance, he looked bewildered and stared steadfastly at Benedict's short left arm and half-hid himself behind Mama's back.

Benedict had noticed.

He crouched down, smiled at Paul and said:

"Looks weird, doesn't it?"

"What's wrong with your arm?" came back promptly.

"Nothing in particular. It's slightly shorter than the other one. I was born that way. It's not so bad."

"Does it hurt?"

"No."

Benedict looked the boy unwaveringly in the eyes—which in turn didn't quite know where to look.

"Are you right-handed or left-handed?" said Benedict.

"I don't know."

"Which hand do you hold the crayon in when you draw a picture? With the right or the left?"

"With this one," Paul said, holding up his left hand.

Benedict held out his own left hand and said: "Good day, young man. I'm Benedict, but you call me Beni."

Paul took his hand and shook it in an exaggerated manner, just as, in his eyes, adults sometimes did. Then Benedict made his grip a little stronger and said in a challenging tone:

"Powerful grip, my boy. Show me how strong you are. Show me what you've got; this isn't everything, right?"

Paul pressed Benedict's hand as hard as he could.

"Great!! You're pretty strong."

Paul looked proudly up at his mother, beaming.

"You see?" Benedict said, "It doesn't hurt me. It's all right, you don't need to be afraid."

Then he straightened up and looked at Yvonne. "To what do we owe this honor?"

Yvonne took the plate with the apple pie from the tote bag. It was covered with two clean napkins that she now removed.

"I behaved badly on Friday, and I've come to apologize."

"That's excellent," said Benedict's father. "I was just about to pour us some coffee." He then set the table with desert plates, forks and coffee cups, which he took from the cupboard. He also brought another glass for lemonade or apple juice for Paul. Yvonne placed the pie on the table and sat with Paul on the bench, to prevent him tipping on the chair. Benedict took a chair, and while his father made the coffee in the kitchen, Yvonne apologized for evicting him so harshly on Friday evening.

"Actually, the logical question would be why you're hiding from reporters, but I have the feeling that you don't want to talk about it," he said. Yvonne just nodded.

Then his father came with a knife and handed it to Yvonne, so that she could cut her pie.

"We don't get many visitors here," he said and then went to the kitchen and got the coffee as well as a bowl of fresh cream which he'd whipped while the water for the coffee was boiling.

The pie wasn't very sweet.

Yvonne had used too little sugar. Without the juicy apple slices and the cream, it would have clearly been too floury. She apologized for it, but the men insisted that it tasted fine, until Paul pushed his plate away and said what everyone knew:

"It doesn't taste right."

First, there was a brief moment of general embarrassment, but then Yvonne began laughing. The two men also laughed, and then Paul joined in and repeated over and over, "It doesn't taste right. It doesn't taste right," because it was obviously the reason for the sudden cheerfulness. When things calmed down, Benedict's father asked, "Where do you come from, and what brought you to Seilersfeld, of all places?" Benedict looked first at Yvonne and then at his father.

"That's the same question I asked her—which led to the coffee table being cleared. She would probably prefer to keep it to herself."

"Does that sound familiar, my son?"

He put his hand on Yvonne's forearm.

"He always wants to know from me what it was like during the war. What I saw and what I did. Obviously, we have something in common, young lady. You don't think I'm going to go out and spread the word to every reporter, right?"

He called her young lady, although as a mother she no longer fit that description. Benedict rolled his eyes.

"Sometimes it's better to talk about things in order to let them go, instead of letting them eat away at you," he said.

"Tell him," the old man prompted Yvonne.

She looked from one to the other and then gazed into the distance. She held Paul close, and her words sounded as if she were talking to herself.

"That sounds so nice: to let things go. But what do you do when those things won't let *you* go?"

"Does that sound familiar to you?" the father asked his son, who answered, clearly irritated, "Let it be. Don't even start with it." Yvonne asked, "Can we change the subject?" Benedict got up and disappeared into the hallway. He could be heard walking up the stairs to the upper floor. Yvonne turned to his father.

"Your son told me you were retired?"

"Yes, for a few years. I was an advisor to the district administration. What do you do?"

At that moment, Benedict came back. He'd brought a small peaked cap with him. As he got closer, Yvonne recognized that it was a train conductor's cap. Benedict went over to Paul and put the cap on his head. Then he took his arm and took Paul off the bench.

"Come, I'll show you something great. You'll like it. For sure." And this time he left the room with Paul. Yvonne cleared the table together with Benedict's father. They brought the dishes into the kitchen, and the former district-administration advisor immediately emptied hot water into the sink. They divided up the work. He washed, she dried. Their conversation was harmless. He wanted to know if Paul had to return to school the next day. She said no, and explained that Paul did not need to attend in the last few weeks before the holidays. She had just enrolled him, although he was already seven. He would start in first grade after the holidays.

When they were finished, they went back into the living room. Benedict and Paul had not returned. Yvonne wanted to know where they were. Benedict's father led her down a steep cellar stairway, and they entered a large dry basement. When Paul saw them, he shouted excitedly, "Mama! Mama! Look!"

A large, thick wooden board was fixed to one wall, and on it she saw the extensive landscape of a Märklin model railway. A steam locomotive with four long green passenger cars came clattering out of a mountain tunnel and entered a long left turn. At the edge of the board a modern express train rode around everything else, and through the center snaked a small freight train that passed through the station of a small town. Small plastic cars, women with prams and men with coats and briefcases populated the streets. At an intersection, a police car with real flashing blue lights was cordoning off the scene of a traffic accident. Paul had never seen anything like this. His enthusiasm and fascination were obvious. He repeatedly readjusted the conductor's cap, and when the steam engine with the green passenger cars approached the station from the other side, he held a signal-paddle with its red side in the air, and Benedict slowed the train with a rotary knob until it came to a halt at the platform. Yvonne heard her son call again: "Everybody off. Everybody off. Please show your ticket," while looking at Benedict.

She tried to imagine him as a child, playing for hours with this train-set and forgetting the outside world. But then she noticed that the setup looked far too new. It could not possibly be thirty years old. His father seemed to read her mind.

"It's mine. I bought it after I retired. It's my passion," he said with his boyish smile.

"Can I start them up again? Please?" Benedict was beseeched by the small and zealous conductor. His father stepped up to the plate and pushed Benedict aside. "I'll show our new engineer how everything works. We'll take a couple of nice trains out for a run. You two can take a walk in the beautiful weather, OK?"

He winked to Yvonne.

"Oh yes, oh yes!" cried Paul. Benedict and Yvonne looked at each other and nodded almost simultaneously.

They took the VW Beetle a few kilometers outside the village to the east, where the forest began. Neither of them had any desire to take a walk in the village itself. Benedict steered off the main road onto a dirt road that led into the woods and parked the car there.

For a while they walked side-by-side in silence until they reached a small, softly-rippling stream that followed the path they were on. Then they came to a point where a second stream cut across the path, and then emptied into the first one. It was quite wide, and someone had laid two narrow planks over it as a sort of bridge. However, it was a shaky, unstable arrangement, and they held hands as they carefully balanced on the two boards. Yvonne secretly wished she had been able to continue holding his hand, but of course he let hers go when they got to the other side. Since their arrival in the forest, they had not spoken to each other. No breeze moved the leaves, and so the trees remained quiet also. There was an occasional buzz in the air, and here and there a brief rustling in the undergrowth, but otherwise the only sounds were their own footsteps and the water when it splashed against stones or roots. The air smelled of sap and moss.

Yvonne was ruminating on a remark that Benedict's father had made while they were drinking coffee: that

Benedict must know the feeling of something that would not let go. It seemed to her as if it had to do with something besides the father's war experiences, something which stood between the two and remained unspoken—despite the usual harmony that seemed otherwise to prevail between father and son.

The path bent to the left and led over a wooden bridge that crossed the stream. It was made of coarse planks and had a railing on either side. In the middle of the bridge Yvonne caught Benedict's arm and pulled him to the right-side railing.

"Let's stay here for a little while," she said, as she put her elbows on the railing and looked down at the smoothly-flowing water. Benedict moved to her side and did the same. Then, after a while, he broke the silence.

"I don't really know how to act," he said quietly. "Things couldn't be better for us to get to know each other. I for one would very much like to get closer to you, but…"

"Me too," Yvonne said immediately, as if someone had stuck her with a needle and released all the internal pressure.

Then he finished his sentence:

"…but it's difficult if you stay silent on everything about yourself; if we can't talk openly."

They looked into each other's eyes, and Yvonne kept her gaze steady, though her lower eyelids began to flutter and soon filled with tears. She knew no way out from her dilemma. She wanted to get to know this man better, she wanted him to enjoy his time with her, to hold her, to give her a little of the strength and security that emanated from him, and she dreamed that he might even one day be able to love her. If she were to remain behind her wall of self-imposed anonymity, she would lose any chance of this happening. If she opened herself up to him instead, he would learn who she really was and what she had done. Then he would despise her, and she would lose him. What's more, she would also have to disappear from Seilersfeld, and she had no idea where she would go. The relationship of her brother with the Holzgärtners had been a godsend.

She felt completely helpless.

She had only two alternatives—to remain silent or to speak—and neither was acceptable.

What could she do?

Her flickering eyelids could no longer contain the flood of tears, and they ran down her cheeks, thick and dark because of her mascara.

Yvonne did not sob, she wept silently.

All this time she continued to look at Benedict, blurred as her vision was, as if she expected to somehow be rescued from her feeling of hopelessness by him.

There was a lot of despair, sadness and fear in her eyes, and Benedict could not tell which of these emotions was the most critical. He turned to her and took her in his arms. He laid her head on his chest and stroked her hair to comfort her. He tried to support her with his weaker arm, because he could feel that her legs were weakening. What in Heaven's name had happened to this poor creature? Now Yvonne began to sob. While her tears still expressed her quiet desperation, she was at the same time overcome by a comforting and consoling feeling, a spark of hope kindled by being held and stroked. Benedict thought he heard Yvonne choking back the words "I can't, I can't" through her sobbing. He took her head in his hands and lifted it. They looked again into each other's eyes, and Yvonne choked back one last faint "I can't."

Then they kissed.

Initially cautious and tentative, then suddenly passionate, and finally tender and exploratory. Neither of them could have said later how long it had lasted until they separated and headed back to the path. This time, however, they went hand in hand, but once again as silent and placid as before. It was only when they came to the rickety boards on which they crossed the second brook that Benedict told her that he didn't care what she'd been through or what she'd done. She didn't have to explain herself.

Then he added: "As far as I'm concerned, there is no past, as long as there is a future for us."

They went the rest of the way home in silence.

7

The next two days were a glorious time for Yvonne. Although she missed Benedict, who'd told her that he'd be on the road Monday and Tuesday, he'd also said that he planned to take off work on Wednesday, so that they could spend the whole day together. She felt so full of energy, and she put it to good use. She did the laundry, cleaned the apartment, swept and dusted. When she went with Paul into Wilma's kitchen, where he wanted to pet the kittens, she helped her landlady to wash up, and even scrubbed the oven. All activities which allowed time for reveries. And when she spied the Monday edition of the *Passauer Neue Presse* in Wilma's kitchen, she had a very good reason to come back the next day.

She sat down at the table and flipped eagerly through the paper, looking for articles that Benedict had written. There was nothing in the Monday edition, since he had had a free weekend. Wilma brought her the Saturday edition, which she had not yet discarded. Yvonne found two articles by Benedict there: an interview with a famous actor and a report on the opening of a large department store on the outskirts of Passau. In it, Benedict also gathered quotes from customers and businessmen from the inner city. There was no general agreement on whether this concept would succeed. The department store had provided a large parking lot, but could not rely on regular customers, as it was relatively far off the beaten path. Some laughed at this foolish project, but Benedict hinted between the lines that he was worried about a massive medium-term drop in sales in the inner city, should this "foolish project" prove successful.

The next morning, she found a report on the first day of the trial of the corrupt Nuremberg building department head. That must have been his assignment the day before. In Nuremberg. That meant he was really there the whole day; he would probably even have to stay in Nuremberg overnight. She wondered whether he would need to attend the second day of the trial today — Tuesday — and report on the verdict tomorrow.

Yvonne had Wilma told what they had done on Sunday, and how the day had gone. She had confessed her love for Benedict and also the fact that he apparently felt the same way. The pressure to express her happiness and to share it was simply too great. The farmer's wife put her arms around her and squeezed her tightly. She repeatedly proclaimed how wonderful it was, and that they both deserved this happiness.

Yvonne was allowed to take Benedict's articles with her once Gustl had read the paper. She read them again and again, if only to be near him in this way. She ran her index finger over the lines while she read and imagined herself having been there while the interviews were taking place. She whispered to herself the questions Benedict had asked the actor, and imagined them sitting in two chairs facing each other, rubbing their chins or emphasizing a question or an answer with an index finger. He was constantly with her for these two days. She thought of him the first thing in the morning when she woke and the last in the evening when she fell asleep. He was there when she was working, when she was playing with Paul and especially when she was just sitting quietly on a bench in the yard watching the normal bustle of the farmyard. She had the feeling that everything had always been predestined. Everything had befallen her was meant to happen, in order that her life would lead her here. To his side.

And all the women whom Benedict might possibly have befriended would have let him go on his way, having sensed that he belonged to another.

To her.

She enjoyed, whatever she was doing, recalling certain details again and again. The blue-white patterned coffee mugs, the ornate chair backs with heart-shaped cut-outs, the wooden stairway in the hall that led up to his world, the narrow planks, on which they had balanced hand-in-hand, his lovingly worried face, blurred behind a veil of tears.

The kisses.

All of it stayed with her. Nothing faded, no matter how small and insignificant something might be in the greater context of worldwide happiness. Everything had its place, and any big picture was inconceivable without the little things that contributed to it. She took all these little things with her wherever she went, whatever she was doing. It seemed as though they changed her bearing, her look, her voice, her smile. And all the while, she kept hearing his voice.

"As long as there is a future for us."

Yes.

She almost managed to forget her fear and guilt for the first time during these two days of waiting, dreaming and constantly going over her memories. But thoughts of the future were accompanied by anxiety. The fear of losing him if he discovered her secret. The fear of being despised and rejected by the love of her life. The fear of all the effort it would take to protect *her* relationship and *her* love from his curiosity, to keep it forever buried with silence and with lies.

Seilersfeld was a small and quiet nest. A peaceful and harmonious patch of earth that managed to set itself up comfortably in a time warp, in which the transition from sunshine to rain or the progression of the seasons were the most significant changes that one noticed.

Everyone knew everyone, everyone was on familiar terms with everyone, everyone knew everyone's history and everyone else's family relationships. And almost everyone in the village, except for the very old, had been baptized by the current pastor. The unchanging sight of milk bottles at the front door, black coal piles in the cellar or stacks of firewood next to the house (depending on which was used to fire the furnace), the familiar clatter of the two-horse wagon on the cobblestones and the smell of wheat, apple trees or the incense on Sunday promised a solid steadfastness of the local life, one that was still remote from that of driving women, of children propped in front of televisions, or of university students who questioned this functional society without ever having done anything for it. Life went along at its own immutable pace, and so it was no surprise that the hysteria—which began at Mechthild Hofreiter's dinner table on Tuesday evening—spread rapidly like a contagious epidemic from door to door, from house to house, from family to family, and finally wound up in the form of several dozen men and women, fathers and mothers (accompanied by their more or less distraught sons and daughters) as a throng gathered in front of the mayor's house, outraged, cursing and ranting.

Of course, Sepp Hirschlsberger, the mayor, wanted to know the reason for this commotion, and initially he struggled to make sense of the explanations being pelted at him from so many mouths. But eventually, he managed.

Marie Hofreiter, the fifteen-year-old daughter of Mechthild and Frederick Hofreiter had told her parents at dinner that a very special rumor had made the rounds on the playground and in the classrooms. Michl Holzgärtner had boasted to the other boys that he had seen that Schmidt woman, who lived in the apartment on his farm, stark naked—but only by chance, when he had work to do in the barn and had looked through a crack in the wall when he heard an unfamiliar automobile drive into the yard, driven by a man who had disappeared into the back of the house with Schmidt. And later the man had handed her money in the parlor. He was dressed only in his underwear, and Schmidt was completely naked.

Marie had added, in a disgusted tone, that when Michl had seen Schmidt, he saw *everything*, even the hair down below, and he wanted to collect money from the other boys for letting them use the barn.

Into this confusion in front of the mayor's house were added different versions of the story by other boys who went to the same district school. Some had heard that Schmidt was only topless, others said they'd heard that she was not naked, but had worn lace underwear, and still others claimed that she had done it with the stranger right in the parlor.

But those boys who were said to have a closer relationship to Michl Holzgärtner, like Berni Kranz, insisted that Schmidt was not naked but was wearing a bathrobe or something similar, and only the white strap of her bra was visible. Furthermore, she didn't have sex with the man—but he *had* given her money in the end; that was true.

It was not clear at this point whether Michl Holzgärtner had embellished and exaggerated the description of his observation in an attempt to collect entrance fees to the barn, or whether Yvonne Schmidt gradually shed her garments only after word got around in the schoolyard more. However, there was agreement among the boys interviewed about the farmer's son—the only one who had actually seen the woman from the barn—that he had claimed that she was wearing nothing, or very little and had gotten money from the stranger.

Mechthild Hofreiter summed things up in a way that they could all agree on. It was irrelevant whether Schmidt had been naked or half-naked. Even in the most harmless descriptions, after all, she was wearing nothing more than a bathrobe. The important point was that every version of the story, from the wildest to the most harmless, contained some recurring and identical details, and in any case led to a single conclusion.

This situation must finally be dealt with.

The entire throng, with the mayor at the head, marched over to the Gruber house. Judge Gruber, being the district magistrate, listened patiently to the evidence, which the mayor earnestly explained, and then replied that this was clearly a commercial sexual offence that in any case could not be permitted in Seilersfeld. When asked what could be done, he went into his house and returned shortly afterwards with a legal tome. He leafed through it until he found what he was looking for.

A fine of five hundred marks or imprisonment was the penalty for anyone who habitually engages in commercial sexual offence in an apartment where children between the ages of three and eighteen live, he announced in an official tone.

This whole affair could be dealt with the next day, he explained to the relieved crowd in front of his house. He turned to one of the fathers, whose brother, he knew, worked at the district's Youth Welfare Office. He instructed him to call his brother the next day from the mayor's office and explain the facts to him. His brother should then request from the court an emergency application for institutional care for little Paul. He himself would then grant this request tomorrow and supplement it with a provisional arrest warrant for Yvonne Schmidt. She would remain in custody until the subsequent process of child custody for Paul had been transferred to the Youth Welfare Office. She herself would most likely be placed in an institution for wayward women, but he could not say for sure at the moment.

In any case, the Youth Welfare Office could still show up tomorrow afternoon, or at the latest on Thursday morning at the Holzgärtners, accompanied by a police car and pick up the boy and his depraved mother. In this way, this unfortunate episode for Seilersfeld would be taken care of.

Almost taken care of, he added somewhat sadly.

Because the Holzgärtners would have to be served with a complaint of procuring. Because of the criminal prosecution, the authorities would not be able to sweep that under the rug.

Benedict returned to Seilersfeld from his assignment shortly before midnight. It was too late to visit Yvonne, so he went directly home. When he opened the door, he was surprised that the parlor light was still on. Normally his father went to bed much earlier. But he wasn't alone. Benedict's skittles friends, the shopkeeper Peter Kranz and the police chief Hubert Förster, had been waiting for him.

They told him in detail what had happened earlier that evening, and what was going to happen the next day under a judicial decision. They said that they, unlike their wives and most of the others, had a bad feeling about it. From Benedict's father they had learned that the woman had been here on Sunday, and because of that they thought he should know about the judge's plans.

Benedict paled.

After his assignment today, he was already upset beyond measure, but what his friends told him just put him in a panic.

A situation he had no idea how to deal with.

"Damn!" he gasped. Then he turned around and ran out of the house. There was no time to lose. What he had to do could not wait until tomorrow. His two friends looked puzzled at first, then they ran after him. Benedict sprinted up the Ludwigstraße and then turned right into the main street. He ran past the old fountain and the yellow phone booth that had been there for two years. Peter and Hubert tried to keep up with him, but they succeeded only with difficulty. Benedict did not stop until he reached the house of Klaus Benscheidt, who was supposed to pass on the judge's instructions to his brother in the Youth Welfare Office the next morning. Benedict rang the bell and pounded his fist repeatedly against the door until it finally opened. Klaus stood before him in his bathrobe, with bright blue pajamas visible underneath.

He was wearing slippers.

Peter Kranz and Hubert Förster caught up now, panting. Benedict said only "Come with me!" and pulled his old schoolmate in bathrobe and pajamas down the steps to the street. Klaus first protested vigorously, but when he realized that even the village police chief was present and was making no attempt to disapprove of Benedict's behavior or to prevent it, he allowed himself to be led by Benedict the few hundred meters to the judge's house. He asked repeatedly what this was all about and what Benedict had in mind. Questions that the other two were also asking themselves.

When the little troop reached the judge's house, Benedict rang the bell and pounded the door once again until the lights came on inside and Judge Gruber appeared in pajamas and bathrobe in the doorway.

"We need to talk!" Benedict said, pressing Klaus past the completely perplexed judge and into the house. Right after that he forced himself past Roland Gruber. And before he could say anything, Peter Kranz and Hubert Förster passed him and followed Benedict. They, however, at least thought to say, "Hello, Roland."

8

The next morning, Benedict awoke with a headache. Yesterday had been long and arduous, but the night, because of his intervention with Roland Gruber, had been short. He had slept little and badly. It was the day of the visit to Berlin of U.S. President Kennedy, and they had sent the rookie from the School of Journalism to Berlin. Whatever.

Benedict was busy with something else.

He longed with every fiber for Yvonne, and he had to speak with her. So he had a shower and a hasty breakfast, then drove to the Holzgärtner farm. His first stop was at the always-open door into the kitchen of the farmer's wife. He explained that he needed to talk to Yvonne for a couple of hours in private, and asked her to look after Paul this morning. Then he went to see Yvonne. He first greeted Paul as the first-rate locomotive engineer. Given Paul's presence, the reunion with Yvonne was not as passionate as both of them had inwardly desired—but they made up for it later on the side of the road in the Beetle.

He wanted to show her something, he said, and drove into the middle of the village. He parked the car right next to the church. Its gold domed tower with the wind gauge on top towered over every house in Seilersfeld and could be seen from anywhere. Benedict took Yvonne's hand and led her around the church, then entered the local cemetery with her. There were a couple of older villagers there, who looked surprised to see them.

The cemetery was well maintained, like every garden and lawn in the village. Even the oldest graves, with their weathered and partly slanted stones from the last century, were looked after so that no weeds grew around them. In the western edge of the cemetery, he stopped in front of one of the gravesites.

"Hi Mom, this is Yvonne. The woman I love."

Yvonne looked at the simple gravestone and read inscription. There was no maxim, not even an introduction in the sense of "Here lies…" or something. The stone bore just the bare data.

Helen Marquardt
Born Springer
3/15/1899 – 12/17/1944

"Hello, Frau Marquardt," Yvonne said, and added softly. "I'm the woman who loves your son."

She had been longing for Benedict for two days, two days that seemed never to end. Why was he bringing her here, to his mother's grave, rather than spending the time on a romantic getaway, a few intimate hours in the woods, or in a town where nobody knew them? Not that she was unwilling to show his mother this kind of respect—especially when it was so obviously on his mind. But she had expected something else for this day.

Opposite the grave was a bench for lingering, and Benedict invited Yvonne to sit there with him. She put her hand on his thigh while he was still looking at his mother's grave for a few minutes. Then he suddenly said: "It's fake. She's not really here."

"I don't understand," Yvonne said.

"There was nothing left of her to be buried," he said. "She died in a bombing raid on Munich on December 17th, 1944. It was a direct hit. Everyone in the building was completely burned. Even my grandmother, my mother's mother."

"I'm so sorry."

"I had this grave dug in 1956, and I pay the rent for it. It contains only a few clothes, photographs and some personal items of hers. My father doesn't like it. He wasn't here when the coffin and the contents was lowered. He was never here. This grave exists only for me. I also paid for the bench we're sitting on."

Yvonne listened to him in silence.

"It took me twelve years to come to terms with my guilt. But then I needed this place, where I could go and sit and talk to her."

Yvonne pricked her ears up.

"Your guilt? What kind of guilt?"

It took a moment before he answered.

"My father was in British captivity since September of 1944. We'd been home alone since then. When Christmas was approaching, I longed to see my grandmother. I suggested that we go to visit her in

Munich in early December and stay until New Year's, but my mother was against it. She wanted to bring her mother to Seilersfeld, because it was safer here than in the big city. I was 18 years old at the time, and had had enough of this wasteland. I didn't just want to see my grandmother, I also wanted to see Munich. To be in the big city. To see the Feldherrnhalle and everything else in the so-called capital of the national-socialist movement. I was a fool, a dreamer, you know?"

Yvonne had not expected this. The picture that she had concocted of Benedict was of a liberal freethinker. A Nazi? Or at least a sympathizer? That was astonishing. But maybe you had to explore all three hundred and sixty degrees, including the dark side, to understand, to be free. Her own life had been far too simple to judge. There was still so much to discover about him.

"Anyway," he continued, "we talked a lot about it and even argued about it. But ultimately, I convinced her. We visited my grandmother in Munich and planned to celebrate Christmas and the New Year with her and then take her with us back to Seilersfeld in early January. That was the compromise. It didn't happen. On the night of December 17th, the bombers came. That evening I was watching the weekly newsreels in a movie theater, and afterwards sat in a bomb shelter. When I returned to my grandma's apartment building after the all-clear signal, it was no longer standing."

Yvonne said nothing, but she patted him consolingly on the back.

"If I hadn't persuaded my mother to go to Munich, we would have brought my grandmother to Seilersfeld instead, and both of them would still be alive. I carried the blame for her death for many years. And when my father came home, at first he felt the same way. But unlike me, he quickly began putting the blame on those who were actually responsible. Politicians who fought the war as they did. Churchill, for example; but first and foremost Hitler. I needed longer to see that my share of responsibility for the death of my mother and my grandmother involved no individual guilt. Somebody decides to take the car and gets into an accident. Somebody decides to take the train, and it derails. The consequences of a decision which have nothing to do with the reasons one made it don't justify any responsibility or guilt. If I create an accident by reckless driving, then I'm responsible. But if I get into an accident through no fault of my own, then I'm not responsible for the accident nor its consequences, just because I chose to take the car instead of the bicycle. I am not responsible for the fact that that bomb hit my grandmother's house and not the theater or the cellar where I was sitting."

Yvonne could not shake the feeling that Benedict had a reason to tell her this story. That he wanted to tell her something through it.

That worried her.

Anything else would have been just a coincidence. That's why she didn't comment while he was telling his story. She had her hands in her lap, staring intently at the grave filled only with personal belongings. Benedict himself paused before he started again.

"The day before yesterday I reported on a trial in Nuremberg," he said.

"I know," said Yvonne. "I read your article in Wilma's newspaper."

Benedict did not ask whether or how she liked it.

He wanted to tell something else.

"Yesterday I was in Ingolstadt, for the public memorial service for the seven kindergarten children who had been shot by a gunman."

Yvonne stared at the empty grave.

"I even interviewed Alfons Goppel, the Bavarian Prime Minister. And also the lead criminal investigator and former colleagues of the perpetrator, who was killed by the police. He was a 40-year-old mechanic from the Auto-Union."

He paused for a moment. Yvonne was still staring at his mother's grave, and seemed suddenly to be lost in her thoughts.

"He had a Russian pistol. A Makarov. They assume that he had brought it back from the war and kept it at home all this time." Benedict turned to the seemingly dreaming woman next to him and spoke to her directly: "Actually, it wasn't his plan to shoot those children, you know?" Yvonne said nothing, and Benedict saw that she was barely breathing. It didn't surprise him, so he went on: "He wanted to shoot only his wife and his son. His boy went to this kindergarten, and his wife was one of the kindergarten teachers."

Benedict reached into the inside pocket of his jacket and fished out the pack of cigarettes. Although he suspected that Yvonne did not smoke, he offered her one. She pulled a cigarette out of the pack. Benedict held out his lighter, but Yvonne had difficulty lighting it.

She was trembling.

Then he lit one up himself. Of course, it was frowned upon to smoke in the cemetery, but by now they were the only people around. Most residents of the village had begun to gather at the Heuslinger Gasthof—which had pretty much the only television set in Seilersfeld— in order to watch the direct transmission of the Berlin visit of John F. Kennedy. Everyone was curious to hear Kennedy's speech. Benedict continued his narrative.

"On the day the killings took place, there had been a Red Cross blood donation organized by the Auto- Union. This mechanic participated because he had a blood donor card and already knew his blood type. While he lay there on the gurney and watched his blood flowing through the transparent tube and into the bag, he was telling the man in charge of the Red Cross unit amusedly that each member of his family had a different blood type. He himself was Type A, his wife O, and his son B. That's not possible, said the Red

Cross man. Yes, it's true, the mechanic insisted. The Red Cross man stood firm, as he had expert knowledge. If he had Type A and his wife O, his son could not have B; those were the indisputable laws of blood-group inheritance. So he must be mistaken. The mechanic said he was absolutely sure that his son had blood type B. In that case, countered the Red Cross man, he was absolutely sure that the boy was not his son."

Benedict drew on his cigarette and looked at Yvonne with a searching and anxious look.

"The man turned as white as the sheets on which he was lying, then as bright red as the Red Cross uniform that the other man wore. He pulled the needle from his arm, jumped off the gurney and disappeared. His colleague on the neighboring bed immediately realized what a devastating mistake the insensitive doctor had just committed, and alerted the police. The officer handling emergency calls that day took too long to grasp the situation, and when a patrol car finally reached the mechanic's apartment, he'd already been there and taken the Makarov and was on the way to the kindergarten, where his son went and where his wife worked."

Yvonne held the smoldering butt of her cigarette between her index and middle fingers; she hadn't drawn a puff or moved it in a long while. A long, curved piece of gray ash protruded into the air of the Seilersfeld cemetery like a steel beam of a bombed-out building, bent by heat. It pointed like a finger at the grave in front of them before falling and crumbling.

"He stormed into the kindergarten and shouted furiously for his wife. Like an unleashed Wildman, he tore open every door, searched for her and screamed constantly. And as one of the other kindergarten teachers, crouching scared behind a desk, said that his wife was not here at the school, but at the doctor's, because the boy had suddenly developed a fever, his pent-up anger erupted into uncontrolled and indiscriminate gunfire."

Yvonne had dropped the rest of her cigarette butt.

She covered her ears and whimpered.

Benedict put his arm around her and held her close. She wanted at this moment to open up and spit out all the poison that had accumulated in her throat. But she couldn't. Maybe she'd done it too many times already.

Now she could only whimper.

And then Benedict heard her whisper something:

"That unfaithful whore has seven innocent children on her conscience. I despise her!"

Benedict grabbed her under the arms and lifted her up, and supported her on the way to the car. The tavern on the other side of the church square was full. Every eye in the main room was surely on the young American president behind the lectern in Berlin, and listening his speech. Benedict was sure that many of them watching Kennedy's speech were also happily looking forward to the arrival of the police and the Youth Welfare Office and the custodianship of Paul and the arrest of his mother.

But that wasn't going to happen.

Neither the police nor the Youth Welfare Office would come. He had seen to that the night he told Roland Gruber and the others what he had learned. He'd had to make that decision alone. Without asking Yvonne first.

It was clear to him that he would have had to reveal her secret and thus to sacrifice her.

Her true identity would get around.

That would happen quite quickly, and she could not stay in Seilersfeld. When they reached his gray VW Beetle, they found a note tucked behind the right windshield wiper. A single word was written on it in thick, red marker.

Murderess.

It had happened really quickly.

Yes, Yvonne had to seek a new sanctuary.

But she would not go there alone.

She would no longer be called *Schmidt*.

She would be called *Marquardt*.

Further Recommendations for you from the
"Movie-Length-Stories" Series:

THOMAS DELLENBUSCH

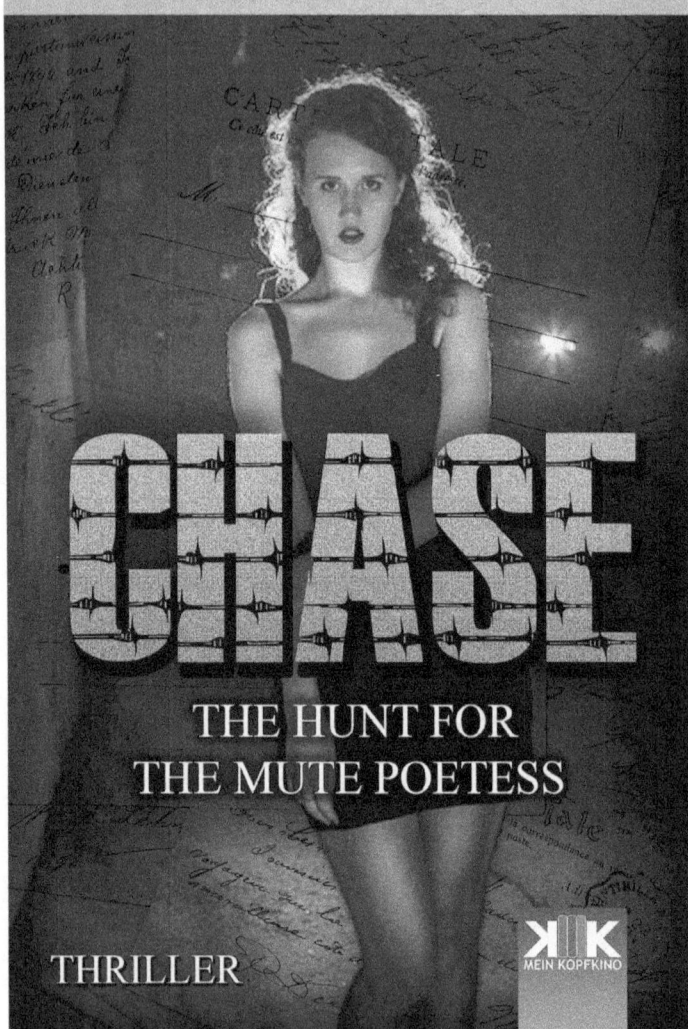

CHASE

THE HUNT FOR
THE MUTE POETESS

THRILLER

K K
MEIN KOPFKINO

Thomas Dellenbusch
"CHASE - The Hunt for the Mute Poetess"

ISBN 978-3-9817967-4-2

Enrique "Rique" Allmers runs a Hamburg security company. When a young woman literally runs into him at the fish market, he protects her from her pursuers. The two of them then flee, but they're already being followed closely. Rique doesn't know who she is or who their pursuers are. He also doesn't know why they're after her. Because she doesn't speak to him...

You genuinely don't know what's going to be the outcome of each encounter – almost every chapter ends with a cracking cliff-hanger. I would immediately have bought the next in the series, and settled in for another 'movie' on the sofa, with popcorn.
Murder, Mayhem & More

Thomas Dellenbusch has written an intriguing crime thriller. I love his fast paced writing style. I would definitely consider reading more books by this author in the future.
Book Reviews by Lynn

Chase... is a fast paced action story. It's taut and well organized, flowing like a movie that keeps you on the edge of your seat. I would personally like to read more of Rique and his teams' exploits.
Books are Theater of the Mind

An exciting caper with well-written action scenes.
Colin Garrow (Scottish Author)

THOMAS DELLENBUSCH

CHASE

THE HUNT FOR A KING

THRILLER

Thomas Dellenbusch
"CHASE: The Hunt for a King"

ISBN 978-3-9817967-9-7

Scotland on the brink of independence: the government is planning its own Scottish monarchy. But when a member of the close-knit planning group reveals the identity of the candidate for the throne, suddenly people appear who want to prevent this royal ascension at all costs - including murder. When CHASE is called in to assist, Jérome and Chen Lu travel to Glasgow. Together with the Scotsman James Campbell, they hunt for his father's murderer. A secretive wax seal leads them into a maze of ancient legends and lost manuscripts. Can they solve the mystery and save the king - or will old ruins become their grave?

If you enjoy historical thrillers like Dan Brown's 'Da Vinci Code' then this CHASE is straight up your street.
Murder Mayhem & More

A pulse pounding ride, with chases, gun fights and several twists that keep a reader hooked.
Book Reviews by Lynn

A super quick, easy and fun read. I'd go so far as to say it would be impossible not to enjoy the book.
David's Book Blurg

Dan Brown goes Kopfkino! Stress, tricky pathways, surprising twists and historical puzzles. This book makes for a heap of fun.
Niliversum

TANJA BERN

Distant Shore
1
Sterne der See

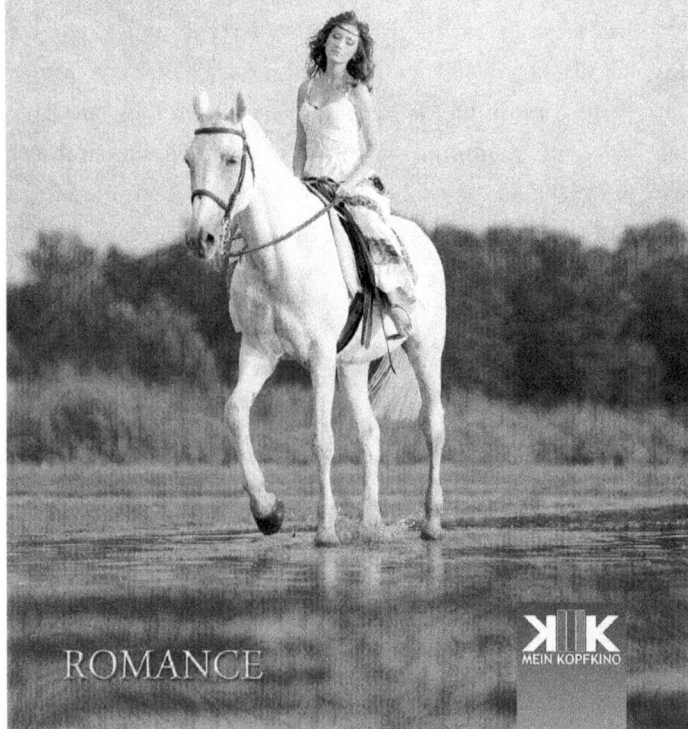

ROMANCE

MEIN KOPFKINO

Tanja Bern
"Distant Shore — Stars at Sea"

Ben has lost his sister Kristin to cancer. Before she died, she'd booked him a holiday in her beloved Ireland, because she suspected that only there would Ben be able to find himself. Although he has no connection whatsoever to Ireland, he decides to make the journey to Kerry. Once there, he meets an Irish girl, Hanna, and is immediately drawn to her. But she's hiding a secret and keeps a certain distance between herself Ben—but then again, she seeks him out. Ben falls in love with this romantic country and loses his heart to Hanna. Then she suddenly goes missing, and Ben does all he can to find her.

Coming Summer/Autumn 2017

I followed the story with a racing heart.
Bücherblog "BuchZeiten"

A rousing romance. Longing in every line.
Bücherblog "Literaturdinge"

I could not put it down.
Melli's Bücherblog

It's one of those books that you don't simply enjoy, but spend the next day thinking about.
Bücherblog "Fairy-book"

Visit us on

Movie-Length-Stories.com

Thomas Dellenbusch was born in Düsseldorf, Germany in 1964, and still lives there. The former police detective and advertising copywriter has been actively writing for more than twenty years on a wide variety of topics. Although the lion's share of his assignments originate from the advertising industry, he has also put his talents to use producing speeches for government officials, poetry for individuals, screenplays, rulebooks, newspaper articles, sketches and much more. In short, any subject that can be communicated in a stimulating manner.

Since 2013, he has specialized in the production of movie-length-stories - written both by himself and seven other authors via the publishing company he founded expressly for that purpose.

www.ingramcontent.com/pod-product-compliance
Lightning Source LLC
Chambersburg PA
CBHW021202020426
42331CB00003B/166